BUCKS COUNTY'S BENEVOLENT SQUIRE
IN SEARCH OF GEORGE FREDERICK TYLER

BUCKS COUNTY'S
BENEVOLENT
SQUIRE

IN SEARCH OF
GEORGE FREDERICK TYLER

DANIEL TYLER

SPRING CEDARS

Published by Spring Cedars
Denver, Colorado
www.springcedars.com

TABLE OF CONTENTS

For my brother Sid,
in recognition of his integrity and gentle leadership of the Tyler Family.

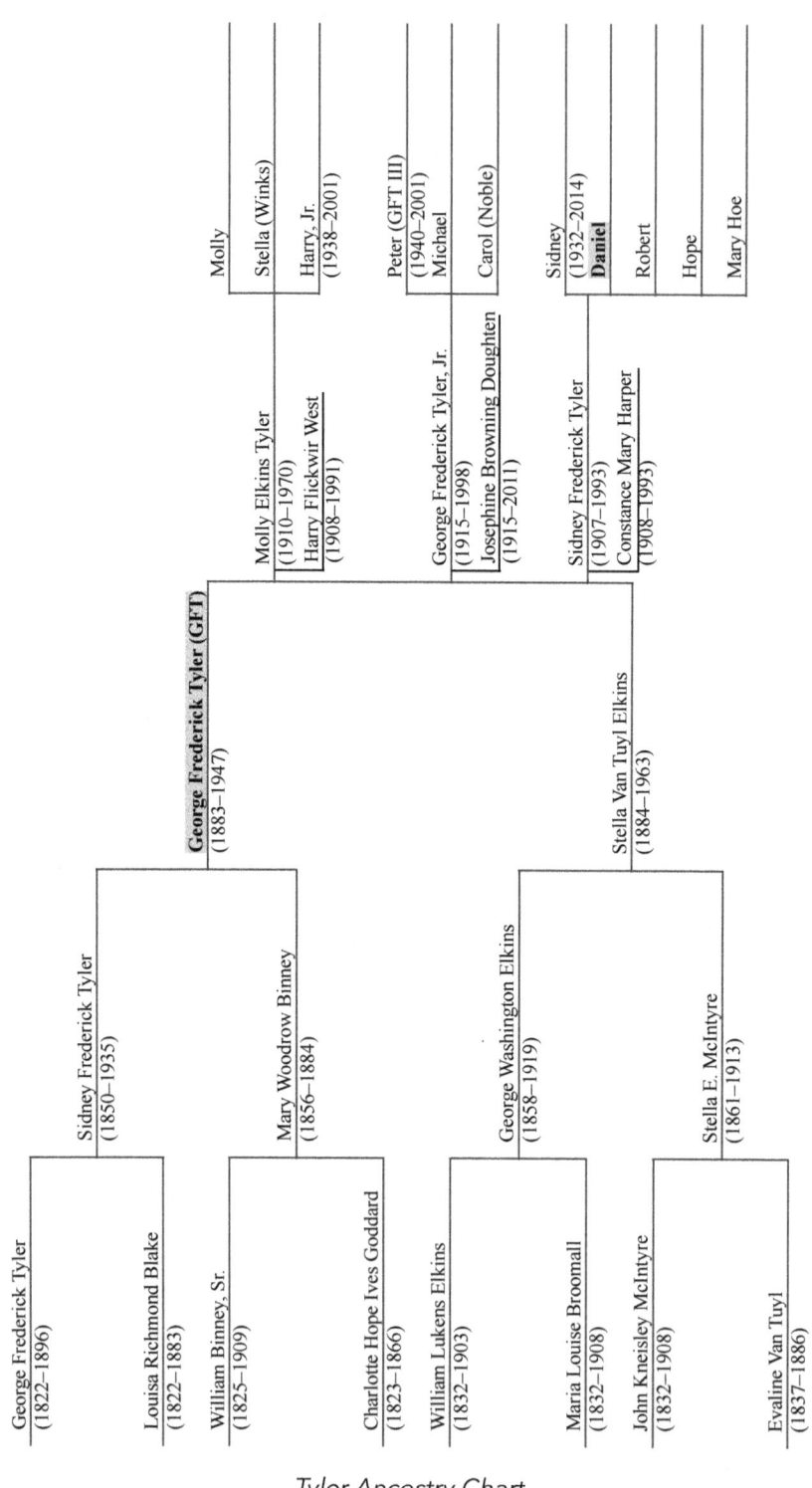

Tyler Ancestry Chart

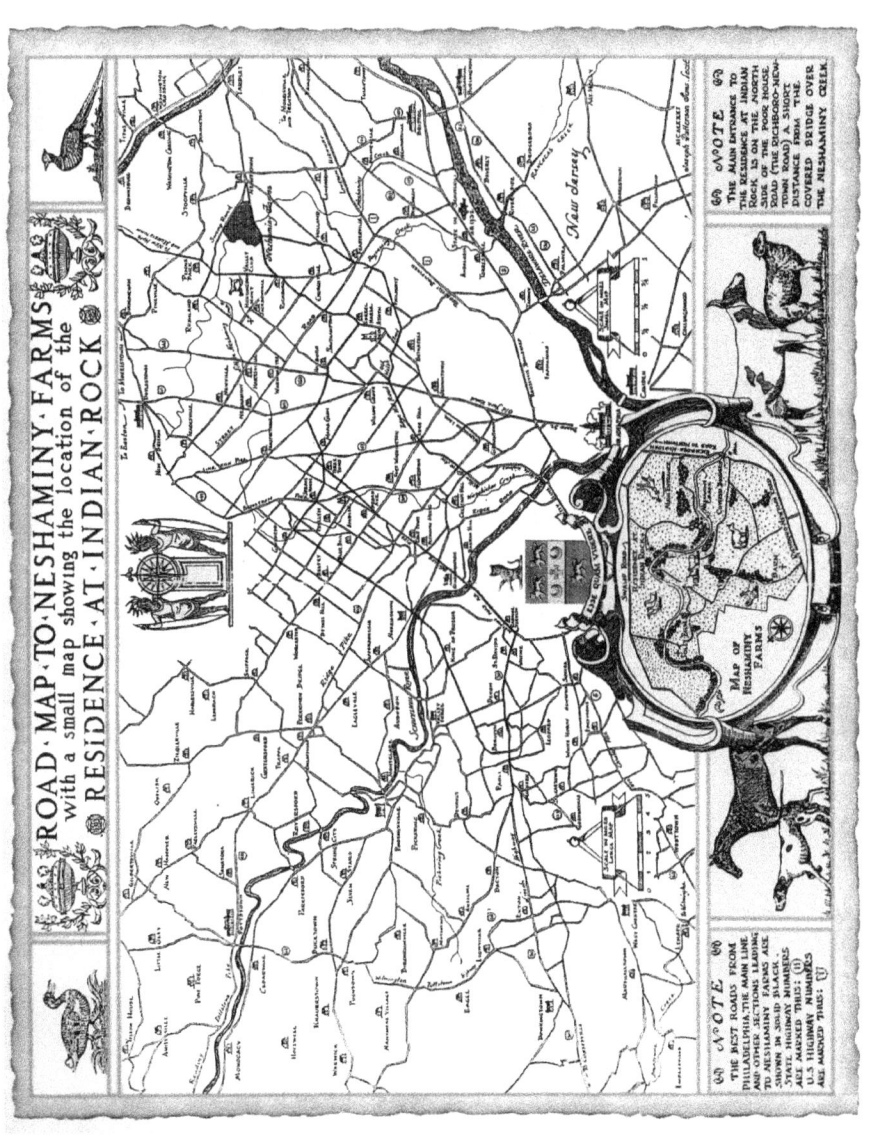

1. Map accompanying invitations sent by the Tylers
for events at their home, Indian Council Rock

INTRODUCTION

My grandfather, George Frederick Tyler, was a mystery to me. I have one recollection of him from 1941 when I was eight years old. My brother Sid and I had just completed a fifteen-mile bicycle trip from our home in Rydal, PA, to my grandparents' mansion: Indian Council Rock in Bucks County, PA. We were enjoying refreshments on one of the outdoor terraces when my grandfather, "Daddy Peter," arrived. He appeared so austere: well-dressed, suit and tie, hair perfectly combed, shoes shined, watch chain hanging down from his vest. A bit scary to me. I don't remember seeing him often during the intervening war years, except for dinner parties at which he was always engaged with his guests and not very welcoming to grandchildren. And within a year of World War II's end, my family was headed to Colorado. No one today recalls how he got the nickname Daddy Peter; he was Petey to other members of his family. But I will refer to him as GFT and to my grandmother, Stella Elkins Tyler, whom her grandchildren called Granny or Dagny, as Stella.

My only other recollection of GFT is in 1947, the year that he died. I was flying back to Massachusetts for the second term of my second year at Brooks School, a boarding school in Andover, MA. Before boarding my flight in Denver, I had been told that GFT was dead. During the fourteen-hour trip to Boston, I tried to experience grief, but I felt nothing. I even sought empathy from a "stewardess" who came and sat beside me, but my feelings of loss were nonexistent. My grandfather remained physically and emotionally a mystery.

Half a dozen years later, Sid and I had a conversation about GFT. We were at Indian Council Rock enjoying time away from college. I don't recall how our discussion began, but I remember Sid saying to me that he had a hard time accepting that our grandparents bought farms; built a sixty-room, French-Norman mansion; and drove around in chauffeured Cadillacs during the depths of the Great Depression. It wasn't like Sid to be critical of family. But his words stayed with me, and when I decided to write about my grandfather, Sid's questions were on my mind. I, too, felt some degree of discomfort about our family's enjoyment of a privileged niche in a society in which the vast majority of Americans were hurting viscerally.

From a variety of sources, I learned that what my brother and I suspected was indeed true. My grandfather purchased somewhere between fifteen and twenty connecting farms in Bucks County, amounting to 2,000 acres of woods and arable land. On a spot overlooking Neshaminy Creek, he built a French-Norman mansion called Indian Council Rock. All around the home, he developed an extensive agricultural operation (Neshaminy Farms) at a time when most of the country suffered from hunger and unemployment. GFT's expenditures for the construction of Indian Council Rock and the purchase of 2,000 acres of farmland at $1,000/acre amounted to $3,361,000 ($57,876,420 in 2021 dollars). It was money spent over the course of several years, during which time hundreds of thousands of people in Philadelphia—a city of 2,000,000 in 1930—lost their jobs, stood in breadlines, and lived in Hoovervilles. At first glance, this data seemed to portray my grandparents as selfish and out of touch with their fellow human beings.

As Nathaniel Burt has noted in *The Perennial Philadelphians*, the center of life for most upper-class Philadelphians was *being* not *doing*. In fact, the very motto on the Tyler coat of arms, *Esse Quam Videri*, translates from the Latin as "To be rather than to seem to be." I have always taken this to mean that one should be honest and true to oneself. But the emphasis is on the *being*, not the *doing*, and both my grandfather, and to a greater extent my father, committed to *doing* something meaningful in life. This sense of purpose separated them significantly from other Older Philadelphians whose motto might have been, "Nothing too much." As Burt points out, among Philadelphia's upper class, "It just wasn't considered good form to be too distinguished." Maintenance of their station, of their sense of position, of their inherited wealth, was at the core of Old Philadelphia's psychological essence.

In this brief biography—by no means an exhaustive study—I want to present a portrait of my grandfather against the background of other similarly privileged Philadelphia families whose inherited wealth placed them in the role of American aristocrats. I want readers to evaluate the extent to which GFT represented the values and activities of that upper class, and how the course of his life also detoured from the lifestyle of others who were "to the manner born." In other words, as someone who was destined by virtue of his birth to have all the benefits of wealth, did GFT also become a man of purpose in search of positive outcomes that would benefit society as a whole? Was he really a *doer*?

In pursuit of answers to brother Sid's and my concerns, there have been plenty of challenges. Originally, I had hoped to present my findings at a family reunion planned for the summer of 2020 in Redstone, CO. I suspect that the younger generations have very little knowledge of their Tyler ancestors, and because we all came into considerable wealth as the result of their business success, it seemed appropriate to present some sort of historical overview that might allow family members to make their own judgments about what went on before and after the Great Depression. Unfortunately, the reunion had to be canceled two years in a row, but the postponements gave me the time I needed to better peel the Tyler family's historical onion.

Research and writing during a pandemic has its limitations. Many questions remain unanswered because I just wasn't able to get the materials I needed from museums, historical societies, archives, and governmental agencies. But those people who assisted me and the websites with which I connected were extremely useful. For anyone interested in following my own path through the various stages of research, I offer a brief summation of my sources at the end of the book. I have decided not to use footnotes. They are distracting. I have made every attempt to reflect accurately the sources available to me.

I also want to note that I have made a considerable effort to determine the size of the Elkins and Tyler estates as they passed down to succeeding generations. Using newspapers and probate records, I have attempted to convert these reported assets into 2021 dollars. The amounts are enormous by any standard. I wanted to include present-day numbers so readers, especially my own family, would be able to understand how and why GFT's descendants have been so fortunate. I feel that an honest appraisal of family wealth and how much stewardship was practiced by several generations of our forebears requires this kind of financial openness.

Not many evaluations or tributes to GFT have survived, and oral testimonials have faded away with the passage of time. Except for the genealogical study he may have sponsored, *The Tyler, Elkins and Allied Families* (New York: Lewis Historical Publishing Company, Inc., 1931), I have not been able to find much writing related to my grandfather. But there are a few contemporary comments about him that have definitely impacted my thinking. They describe a man I wasn't prepared to know.

In a three-volume work entitled *A Joyful Odyssey*, my father wrote about his life and his own family experiences. In the first volume he referred to GFT as being the life of the party before he contracted a kidney disease in World War I. He loved hosting gatherings at his home. He enjoyed fox hunts, sailing, and had a host of friends. He was "universally loved," my father wrote, but he dreaded speechmaking. Roland Porter, Neshaminy Farms' business manager of forty years, said that "Mr. T was the finest kind of man to work for you ever saw. He entered into every aspect of the affairs of the farm." Orville Reeves, the stable master, thought his boss was wonderful, too. When he confessed that his daughter was expecting and needed help, GFT paid for all medical expenses as well as the back operations Orville needed at a later time.

When I shared my somewhat confused and prejudiced

view of GFT with Lyle Rosenberger, Bucks County Community College's talented historic preservationist, he emailed the following to me: "I truly believe that after you examine the materials which I sent you that you will find that George was a very decent human being, always understated. He was someone who had a lot of talent and shared with the community in which he lived in many small and meaningful ways. George, as a person, related well to the locals. He was never boastful and took on the mantle of leadership with humbleness. The mere fact that he was chairman of many local institutions, such as the Abington Memorial Hospital for many years, speaks for itself. I believe that everyone in the Tyler family today can be proud of his personal and genuine touch. He left the world a better place."

So much for the feelings of mystery. Now, to the evidence!

CHAPTER I:
Elkins and Tyler Families

It is difficult to imagine a more financially fortuitous marriage than that of George Frederick Tyler and Stella Van Tuyl Elkins on April 27, 1905. Both families were among the wealthiest Old Philadelphians. Their respective patriarchs had been enormously successful in business during the post-Civil War industrial expansion. They had invested in the extraordinary economic growth of that period, and in the process helped to create a Philadelphia aristocracy that was equal to that of Boston and New York. They took risks during a time of peace when development of natural resources was viewed as the avenue to wealth. When two families with the same philosophy of economic adventurism succeeded and merged in marriage, they entered an upper class with an astounding level of power and prestige.

The Elkins story is one of talent, hard work, and seizing opportunities. William Lukens Elkins (WLE), born in 1832 near Wheeling, West Virginia, had minimal formal education and started his working career as a teenage clerk in a grocery store. His father had experienced success in the paper industry, but WLE began his own business career as a commission merchant in the produce business, buying and selling food for others. He also developed a primitive technique for food refrigeration and was soon able to form his own grocery company, Saybolt and Elkins, which became the largest enterprise of its kind in the United States.

2. William Lukens Elkins, 1832–1903

With the growth of oil production in Northwest Pennsylvania, and concurrent developments in gasoline-powered internal combustion engines, Elkins recognized another opportunity. He formed Monument Oil Works, drilled a lot of exploratory wells, and built a primitive oil refinery. Following the discovery that coal oil could be refined into kerosene for illumination, he began organizing companies that could sell the refined product to consumers. He also may have been the first to refine gasoline in the United States, and he wasn't far behind in the manufacture of petroleum-based asphalt. In 1875 he entered into a partnership with Standard Oil, becoming a significant shareholder.

In 1873, Elkins met Peter A. B. Widener, who had made a lot of money selling mutton to the Union army during the Civil War. The two men became good friends and better business partners. Together they addressed the growing transportation problems of major cities where steam-driven cable cars were proving inadequate for the burgeoning populations. They developed the first system of electric trolleys in 1892 and followed this in 1901 with the organization of the Philadelphia Rapid Transit Company. Their successes were exponential, but they also experienced worker discontent, occasional strikes, and financial difficulties. Nevertheless, Elkins and Widener took their model of electrified trolleys to Chicago, Baltimore, Pittsburgh, New York, Cincinnati, and St. Louis. They came to be known as the "traction magnates." As a result of their accomplishments, they were invited to serve on a variety of business, industrial, and financial boards, which in turn opened doors to more lucrative opportunities and investments.

As Nathaniel Burt in *The Perennial Philadelphians* and E. Digby Baltzell in *Philadelphia Gentlemen* have observed in their respective books about Philadelphia's turn-of-the-century aristocracy, service on the boards of business, financial, and social organizations was not only a badge of acceptance, it was for many the ultimate achievement. Being on boards was the locus of real prestige and power. Some boards were the springboards to other boards. For many boardmen, Burt notes, membership was their real career, "their professional and business success a mere prelude to this final enthronement."

In the last decade of his life, Elkins took advantage of these opportunities. He was much more than a boardman, however, having proved himself the consummate entrepreneur and land developer, purchasing tracts north of Philadelphia where he and Widener built thousands of homes. Because of his many and varied interests, his leadership was avidly solicited by municipal transportation companies, railroads, utilities, trust companies, insurance companies, etc. At the time of his death in 1903, he was serving on a total of twenty-four boards, including the famous Girard estate and the Pennsylvania Railroad.

Elkins was a *doer*, setting a standard for generations of Old Philadelphians who *created* the wealth that would be preserved by succeeding families as a way of life. He belonged to all the right clubs, accumulated dozens of valuable pieces of art, and his assets were responsible for the construction of at least three homes (Elstowe Manor, Chelten House, and Georgian Terrace) in an area that came to be known as Elkins Park in 1898. He was a vestryman at St. Paul's Episcopal Church and donated generously to hospitals, orphanages, and other worthy causes. He married well (Maria Louise Broomall) and had two sons and two daughters: George, whom we will follow next, and William; Ida and Eleanor. When he died in 1903, according to probate information provided in Philadelphia's *Evening Public Ledger*, he was worth \$31,578,268 (\$500,000,000 in 2021 dollars). And that probated amount does not include trusts, insurance policies, property legally owned by partnerships, corporations, limited liability companies, etc. The amount WLE passed on to his heirs, therefore, could easily surpass a billion dollars in today's currency.

Son George Washington Elkins (1858–1919), the future father of Stella Van Tuyl Elkins, added significantly to this cache. He was first educated by private tutors in Philadelphia and then attended Episcopal Academy, extending his learning with summer trips to Europe. When his father died, he was primarily engaged in managing the estate, and because of his nearly automatic admission to Old Philadelphia's inner sanctum, he was appointed to many of the same company boards on which his father had served. He was a director of the Land Title and Trust Company, the Philadelphia Traction Company, and the Metropolitan Street Railroad Company of New York City. He was elected president of the Elkins Gas and Coal Company, treasurer of the Elkins Manufacturing and Gas Company, and trustee of the Hahnemann Hospital. In addition to these positions, he served on the boards of several utilities and construction companies, and was one of the original founders of the Philadelphia Stock Exchange. He was an active philanthropist, being one of the founders of Abington Memorial Hospital, where my siblings and I were born, and his interest in art led him to establish a \$500,000 endowment for the Philadelphia Art Museum. Like his father, he belonged to the "right" clubs and spent much of his leisure time enjoying his yacht, *Juniata,* and golfing with friends at the

Philadelphia Country Club, where he died in 1919 after experiencing a stroke on the 12th tee box. According to observers, he had just started his swing when he collapsed and lost consciousness. Attempts to revive him in the clubhouse failed. He was only sixty-one. Unfortunately, it was the kind of stroke for which there is no mulligan.

3. George Washington Elkins, 1858–1919

George had married Stella McIntyre in 1881. She died in 1913. Four years later, George married the widow Allethaire Ludlow Crummer. All four of George's children were by his first marriage. Stella Van Tuyl Elkins was his second child and the one who married GFT on April 27, 1905. The marriages of Old Philadelphia males to the sisters of other Old Philadelphia males was a common occurrence and resulted in the linking of large fortunes. When George died in 1919, he was worth forty million dollars. Stella was willed one quarter of that family estate, approximately $10,000,000 ($166,200,000 in 2021 dollars).

So much for the Elkins contribution; now, to the Tylers.

We start with my great-great-grandfather, George Frederick Tyler, not to be confused with GFT, my grandfather. He was born in 1822 in Brooklyn, Connecticut, and died in Philadelphia in 1896. He was the grandson of Daniel Tyler, also of Brooklyn, who had buried 3 wives, fathered 21 children, had 50 grandchildren and 120 great-grandchildren, and is one of few Americans able to claim that he had lived in three centuries (1699–1801). George went to work at a dry goods store in New York at the age of seventeen. He became a partner in the coal shipping business of H. D. Sharpe and Co., selling his interest in 1843. Four years later he moved to Philadelphia, where he established a coal mining and shipping business called F. Tyler & Co. He was an early director of the First National Bank of Philadelphia, the National Life Insurance Company of the United States, and the Fidelity Insurance Trust and Safe Deposit Company of Philadelphia. He was president and/or director of several railroad and steamship companies as well as financial houses, and he helped finance the construction of the Bullitt building in Philadelphia where the Fourth Street National Bank was eventually located. George was also a founder of Anniston, Alabama, where he remained involved in all the local industries.

4. George Frederick Tyler, 1822–1896, seated with his family (Hope stands behind her grandfather, with Uncle Harry Black Tyler and Aunt Nellie. GFT sits on his grandfather's lap.)

As strange as it may seem, Old Philadelphians had a close relationship with the South, which in Nathaniel Burt's words, they viewed as "reckless, ruined, but oh how romantic." Along with Old Philadelphia's fascination with all things English, the South was something of a black-sheep cousin with which marriages were regularly consummated across the Mason-Dixon Line. George retired from active business in 1865 and spent summers at 5 Bellevue Court in Newport, Rhode Island.

From his marriage to Louisa Richmond Blake, George Frederick Tyler had four children, one of whom was Sidney Frederick Tyler, GFT's father, who was born December 23, 1850. Like his father, Sidney was first educated by private tutors and then attended the Episcopal Academy on the Main Line in Newtown Square. He entered the sophomore class of Harvard in 1869, the first of four consecutive generations of Tylers in Cambridge. He graduated in 1872 and spent the next three-and-a-half years in Europe. When he returned, Sidney studied law in the office of George W. Biddle and was admitted to the bar in 1878. His first position was as general agent with the Connecticut Mutual Life Insurance Company, which assigned him both Rhode Island and Massachusetts as his territories. He lived briefly in Providence and then moved to Boston. In 1880, he married Mary Woodrow Binney of Providence. Three years later, GFT was born in Newport, Rhode Island, at the summer residence his father had established many years earlier. He was Sidney's second child, the first being Charlotte Hope, born in Boston in 1881. Curiously, there is no record of GFT's birth in Newport Vital Records.

5. Sidney Frederick Tyler, 1850–1935

When Mary died in 1884, Sidney moved back to Philadelphia where, with several others, he organized the Fourth Street Bank of Philadelphia. In 1888, he married Ida Amelia Elkins. In all likelihood, this was not an arranged or consanguineous marriage. But it would have been joyously approved by both families as a means of preserving their wealth and their Old Philadelphia status. Sidney and Ida had no children, but their union merged a stream of assets that reached Olympian heights. Although Sidney was one generation younger than William Lukens Elkins, the older man had such confidence in him that he designated Sidney the executive trustee of his estate when he died in 1903. One stipulation in the will related to how the Elkins money was to be invested. Because William Lukens Elkins had no faith in the stock market, Sidney was required to invest only in oil and tobacco.

In addition to managing the Elkins' estate, Sidney's whirlwind life revealed him to be an exemplary disciple of Philadelphia's gentry. He dotted all the *i*'s and crossed all the *t*'s. He was director, president, or board member for dozens of firms, managing the extrapolation and development of natural resources, including coal, iron, water, coke, gas, and ammonia. He was charged with the reorganization of several railroads, and he served on the board of the Baldwin Locomotive Company. He was director of trust companies, banks, the Standard Steel Works, several water power companies, a munitions company, utilities, and urban transit systems. Following his father's lead, he further developed the Alabama relationship, organizing the Anniston Land and Improvement Company and the Anniston Atlantic Railroad Company. He served a term as president of the Asphalt Company of America, and at the time of his death he was still director of the Fidelity Philadelphia Trust Company, Baldwin Locomotive Works, Standard Steel Works, Philadelphia Electric Company, Philadelphia Electric Power Company, Susquehanna

Power Company, Susquehanna Electric Corporation, Baldwin Southwark Corporation, etc.

And he still made time for other interests. He was on the Committee of the Sound Money League, whose objectives were to restore bullion as backing for the nation's currency and to maintain a high protective tariff. He was a member of the Pennsylvania Society of the Sons of the Revolution, the Colonial Lords of Manors of America, and the Pennsylvania Society of Founders and Patriots of America. He was a member of the Society of Colonial Wars and the Genealogical Society of Philadelphia. He was a trustee of the Polyclinic Hospital of Philadelphia, a life member of the Society to Protect Children from Cruelty, and a manager of the Philadelphia Orthopedic Hospital. He was a vestryman of St. Paul's Episcopal Church and served as a delegate to the annual convention of the Protestant Episcopal Diocese of Philadelphia. He was in every sense the quintessential Old Philadelphian.

Sidney F. Tyler died in 1935. In contrast to George Elkins, he lost his life while attending a board meeting of the Fidelity Philadelphia Trust Company. He was a compulsive workaholic, living out his final years at the St. James Historical Annex in downtown Philadelphia, where he could be close to financial and business activities. At eighty-five, he had far outlived the average life span of a white male born in the United States in the 1850s. He had good genes, which he seems to have passed on to future generations. That said, his only son, my grandfather GFT, died at sixty-three after a life that contrasted notably with that of his father.

Sidney F. Tyler's life epitomized a generation of perennial Philadelphians whose work and play involved the maintenance and growth of a nest egg that had been created by the imagination and resourcefulness of an earlier generation. And through clubs, education, social organizations, marriage, and recreational pursuits, he made sure that he was solidly entrenched in that class of Old Philadelphians, whose goal was to preserve for their offspring the same privileged status they and previous generations so thoroughly enjoyed.

At the time of his death, Sidney F. Tyler's estate was valued at a paltry $200,000 according to a court probate reported in the *Philadelphia Inquirer* and the *Delaware County Daily Times* on June 13, 1935. But on May 30, 1917, Sidney had established a living trust, leaving the bulk of his wealth to his two children: GFT and Charlotte Hope Montgomery. The assets therein were exempted from probate; his will specifically stipulated that his executors "shall not file an inventory, appraisal or an account of my estate in any public office or court and an account stated by my executors shall be accepted by the beneficiaries as a correct accounting and valuation of my estate and no proceeding shall be had requiring the filing thereof in any public office." His son, GFT, and son-in-law, Robert T. Montgomery, were named executors. Newspapers were forced to estimate his real wealth and they guessed he was probably worth at least several million dollars. Additionally, he left $7,500 ($153,750 in 2021 dollars) to his secretary and $1,500 ($31,500 in 2021 dollars) each to his chauffeur and valet.

George Washington Elkins and Sidney Frederick Tyler, fathers respectively of Stella Van Tuyl Elkins and GFT, were contemporaries, born only eight years apart in the 1850s. Sidney was older and he lived longer. But the two men had a lot in common, and what they passed along to their offspring was a set of Victorian values that had been refined by an American plutocracy whose wealth was based on business and finance. As Nathaniel Burt points out, those family firms bound by a holy trinity of coal, iron, and railroads have been most indigenous and most connected to other Old Philadelphians. This was the core of Philadelphia's nineteenth-century industrial prosperity and the basis of most of Philadelphia's nineteenth-century wealth. In their vast estates, homes, and gardens, with miles of driveway leading to craggy mansions, they lived in isolation from the rest of Philadelphia and were able to create and massage the illusion that they were really country folk, while appearing to ignore the ugliness and contradictions of the industrial civilization that supported them. With enormous trust funds, savings accounts, and productive real estate, they were able to focus on their boards and clubs, relieved from the countinghouse and the shop, ready to travel, buy art, learn about horses and wine, give lavish parties, and cultivate the art of charm. Their family members and acquaintances were prominent in the *Social Register* and *Who's Who*, and friends were known more by who they *were* than what they *did*. They were tradition-directed and sought conformity amongst themselves in boardrooms and drawing rooms. They were a moneyed, rather than a political or landed, aristocracy, and they worked tirelessly to undergird their status.

For the next generation, that of my grandparents, this Weltanschauung experienced certain modifications, but the core way of life they embraced gave echo to patterns and priorities already established by their parents and grandparents.

CHAPTER II:

The Early Years to World War I

Although his mother, Mary, died less than a year after he was born, GFT never lacked for care and companionship at home. For the first few years of his life in Elkins Park, he and older sister Charlotte were attended by servants and nannies. By the time GFT reached the age of four, Ida Amelia Elkins had become his stepmother.

It's not known where GFT took his first years of schooling, but it is likely that his father brought in tutors so he could learn in the comfort of familiar surroundings. This was a custom followed by many upper-class families, even through high school years and in some cases through the equivalent of college. If he did attend a private day school, it was likely the Episcopal Academy, as most upper-class Philadelphians were Episcopalians. The Academy, founded in 1785, emphasized the study of classical languages, religion, and mathematics. In 1900 it was located in central Philadelphia, not far from the city's most fashionable Episcopal Church, St. Mark's. Other schools he might have attended were located in Germantown and Chestnut Hill, but wherever he went, he was sufficiently prepared and socially acceptable at the age of twelve for admission to St. Mark's School in Southborough, Massachusetts. With a father who was obsessed with business and a stepmother whose social obligations demanded enormous amounts of time, it was a foregone conclusion that GFT would be sent away to boarding school as soon as he became eligible.

St. Mark's was established in 1865 as one of the first New England boarding schools. It was modeled on Harrow School in London, which dated back to a royal charter granted by Queen Elizabeth in 1572. It took several decades for St. Mark's to establish financial and academic credibility in the United States, but by 1894, when William Greenough Thayer was hired as headmaster, St. Mark's was on its way to attracting the sons of elite families from Boston, New York, and Philadelphia.

Thayer had earned his spurs while teaching at Groton under Endicott Peabody, an ordained Episcopal priest who had attended and admired the English boarding schools. Thayer was still in his late twenties when he arrived at St. Mark's having embraced Peabody's emphasis on moral leadership and philanthropy over intellectual achievement. He rated student applicants not on their skills but on their parents' timeliness in registering their sons for admission. His stated objective was to convert students into Christian gentlemen. Success was in no small part due to his personality and character, which set the tone for the school and created a relationship with students who worshipped him as a venerated father figure.

It's hard to know why GFT's father chose St. Mark's over Groton or the better known St. Paul's or St. George's. But it is conceivable that Thayer's fresh and inspiring leadership might have played a significant role in the choice. Articulate, passionate, and sincere, Thayer was able to put the school on a solid financial footing. By the time GFT arrived in 1895, all beds were spoken for.

From available evidence, it appears that GFT's six years at St. Mark's were reasonably successful. He certainly would have enjoyed the friendships and sports. Eventually, he captained the baseball team, achieving a very respectable batting average of .368. He also played on the tennis team and participated in the school's dramatic productions. For six years he traveled back and forth between Philadelphia and Southborough, Massachusetts, with William Elkins. GFT and William must have tolerated Thayer's increased emphasis on religion, the cold baths they had to take six out of seven nights of the week, and the hazing that sometimes got out of hand. They respected Thayer's desire to have students police themselves in the manner of Eton College and Harrow School of England—both well known for a very strict style of discipline that was often administered by the older students—even though the peer-administered discipline occasionally became physical and punitive. As a result of Thayer's leadership, they were also exposed to uplifting lectures on the importance of public service and were encouraged to discuss progressive issues such as women's suffrage and the value of outreach missions to the less fortunate. They reveled in the school's emphasis on competitive sports—football, baseball, hockey, fives (handball), tennis, and golf—accompanied Thayer to Southborough town meetings to learn about problems facing real people, and cobbled together a decent enough academic record to be accepted into Harvard's Class of 1905. They were in good company at St. Mark's. Of the 34 members of their class of 1901, 27 went to Harvard, 3 to Yale, 2 to Columbia, 1 to Princeton, and 1 to Lowell Technological Institute.

The extent to which Thayer's spiritual and progressive leadership impacted GFT and William Elkins is unknown, but he was seen by both men as a family member, and when it came time for each to get married, Thayer was asked to perform the ceremonies. What are now referred to at St. Mark's as the Tyler Faculty Lounge and the Elkins Field House suggest that both families maintained an ongoing affection for the school that has continued up to the present day.

Harvard was not an automatic college choice for upper-class Philadelphians. Princeton—especially after 1910—and the University of Pennsylvania were favored at the turn of the century, the former because of its setting similar to the lush environs of Chestnut Hill and the Main Line, while the latter was noted for its graduate schools of law and medicine. However, Harvard was older (1636) and more glamorous. Although it was considered somewhat exotic, in the words of Nathaniel Burt, it was also "precious, quaint and tarred with radicalism." Students of privilege who had attended New England boarding schools were not looking for careers when they matriculated at Harvard; they were in Cambridge for the connections they would make and for the status that a Harvard degree would signify amongst their social, financial, and business acquaintances.

Compared to students from public schools, boarding school students at Harvard tended to demonstrate less intellectual rigor. In his book *Philadelphia Gentlemen*, E. Digby Baltzell discusses a study conducted by Charles McArthur of the Office of Tests at Harvard, who discovered in the 1940s a distinct difference in values between the two groups. While public school students focused on the *future*, the *individual*, and *doing* as their principal values, the private school students valued the *past*, the *group*, and *being*. For example, the public school boys made A's in chemistry;

the private schoolers were happy with what have been termed gentleman's C. They saw no shame in just getting by. Academic excellence was not, in most cases, a goal of young men who were more interested in social relationships than in academic performance. Public schoolers came to Harvard with a career in mind; the *being-* and *past*-oriented young private schoolers drifted into the humanities. "Private school attendance," Baltzell notes, "clearly differentiated the members of the upper class from the rest of Philadelphia elite in the 1940s." Those whose parents came from old money, who knew each other in the same clubs and boards and social gatherings, tended to segregate themselves from students whose parents were considered nouveaux riches. GFT seems to have avoided this stereotype, but he still shared a lot in common with those who enjoyed a similar private school education and an upbringing based on whom you knew.

At Harvard, the separation between public and private school students was driven deeper by the existence of final clubs (fraternities) that competed for members who came from the same backgrounds, significant wealth, and *Social Register* parents. Perhaps the most elite club was the Porcellian, to which Theodore Roosevelt had belonged in 1880. But the Fly Club, to which his cousin Franklin Delano Roosevelt belonged, did not lag far behind in prestige. GFT joined the Fly. It had been chartered as an eating club, the Alpha Delta Phi, in 1837, but it was known informally as the Fly since 1885. It went through several charters during the remainder of the 19th century, and by 1910 it became officially The Fly Club. The tradition of Tylers at the Fly continued for three more generations.

G.F.Tyler W.M.Elkins R.D.Humphreys E.Bell H.Peabody B.S.Prentice C.Bigelow
H.C.de Rham P.Lorillard U.A.Murdock E.F.de Rham F.D.Roosevelt W.S.Godfrey S.N.Hinckley W.H.Bradley G.O.Winston E.C.Hovey P.O.Mills
G.C.Lord A.G.Rotch G.S.Barton L.Brown A.F.Bigelow A.M.Brown S.Waller C.B.Bradley G.D.Boardman
G.Williamson   B.S.Litchfield   A.E.Harding   C.P.Bailey

6. The Fly Club, Class of 1904
(GFT top left, FDR second row fifth from left)

The Fly was home for GFT. He took at least one meal a day there, enjoyed friendships with others whose lives paralleled his, and benefited from contact with graduates—already established in business—who returned to the club for special dinners and events, such as the Harvard-Yale game. It was a comfortable social milieu. He could have isolated himself completely in that space, removed from the rest of the student body for his entire time in Cambridge. But he didn't. Like FDR, a year ahead of him, who gave most of his time to *The Crimson* newspaper, GFT became involved with activities outside the club. He was manager of the 1904 football team and played right field on the baseball team. He also joined the Hasty Pudding Club, which had a diverse membership across the college. There's no way to know how involved he was, but The Pudding was a venerable institution, the third oldest theater organization in the world, with a reputation for making fun of just about everything. A patron for the arts and comedy, and an advocate for satire and discourse as tools for worldwide change, The Pudding was the oldest social club in the USA. It has been a cornerstone of the Harvard experience for over two centuries.

7. 1904 Harvard Football Team (GFT far right)

GFT's academic record was mediocre. He was not yet 18 when he began his Freshman year, and his transcript shows that he struggled at first. He took mostly languages, English, history, government, and economics. For the most part, he received gentleman's C, but there were enough D's along the way to prompt an admonishment from the college in the spring of 1903.

By the end of his junior year in 1904, he had accumulated 180 credits, enough to graduate.

GFT did not remain in Cambridge for what would have been his senior year. With all requirements completed, he switched his attention to Stella Elkins. They had developed a strong friendship during GFT's St. Mark's years as a result of the camaraderie between Stella's brother, William, who also attended St. Mark's, and GFT. But their connection all but evaporated when Stella disappeared to France for two years. The hiatus resulted from Stella's opposition to Philadelphia's debutante scene. Instead of attending fancy coming-out parties, according to my father's recollections in *A Joyful Odyssey*, at the age of 17, she and her parents agreed that an acceptable alternative would be for Stella to attend a finishing school in France. Dieudonné, on the outskirts of Paris, was recommended by friends from New York. It was known to have a student body made up largely of American and British ladies. Courses were offered in history, foreign languages, and art, all of which were taught in French. The couple who ran the school had an apartment in Paris and a country home, the Château d'Osny, near Pontoise, twenty miles northeast of Paris. It was the perfect alternative for a shy young lady who was bored by the thought of debutante revelry and abhorred the prospect of having to participate in the annual Philadelphia marriage mart.

Stella's two years in France (1901–1903) were among the happiest of her life. She fell in love with French art, learned to speak French fluently, developed her considerable talents on the piano, and cultivated a real affection for the de Reiset family, who

8. Stella Van Tuyl Elkins at seventeen, 1901

ran the school. She returned home a more mature and refined young lady whose exceptional qualities were immediately apparent to a more cultivated and mature GFT. Over the next year and a half, GFT and Stella experienced an intense courtship, and on April 18,1905, less than a month after Stella turned 21, GFT applied for a marriage license. Because she had barely reached the legal age for marriage, GFT needed a third party to vouch for her at City Hall. Noting on the license application that he had no occupation, GFT secured a license for a wedding that took place on April 27, 1905.

This merger of the Tyler and Elkins families was a coming together of two of the most established, powerful, wealthy, and influential Philadelphia families of the pre-World War II era. If ever a marriage appeared auspicious based on the resources available, this was it. No serendipity here! Their union occurred because their families were so integrated and their upper-class pathways so parallel. Stella married her aunt's stepson; GFT married the niece of his stepmother.

After a honeymoon trip to Europe that featured the people and places Stella had come to know during her stay in France, the couple returned home to Philadelphia, taking up residence in an apartment they called Poverty Flat. As a wedding present, Stella's father, George Elkins, gave them ten acres on the northwest corner of the Elkins Park estate, an old apple orchard, on which he oversaw the construction of a fifty-room "cottage," which took the name Georgian Terrace. This was one of three homes Horace Trumbauer designed for the Elkins family; Elstowe Manor and Chelten House were the other two. Georgian Terrace was constructed in the shape of a capital E and was large enough to house a good-sized family with plenty of servants. Later, when GFT and Stella were well established at their Indian Council Rock home, they gifted Georgian Terrace and the surrounding grounds to Temple University to be used as the first location of the Tyler School of Art and Architecture.

Speculation exists that GFT might have decided to attend

9. Georgian Terrace

Harvard Law School while Georgian Terrace was being built. He noted in the *Twenty-Fifth Anniversary Report* of the Harvard Class of 1905 that he was employed at the Philadelphia firm of Montgomery, Clothier & Tyler from 1907 to 1917. If so, he could have been in Cambridge for a semester prior to commencing work at Montgomery, Clothier & Tyler. He would have taken classes in contracts, property, torts, criminal law, and civil procedure. University law schools, in general, were gaining acceptability over the nineteenth-century approach to the study of law that focused on apprenticeships in legal practice. Harvard's reputation as a law school improved significantly when professors began using the case method based on the idea that law could be studied as a science, an approach that was distinct from vocational preparation. But there is little evidence that he attended at all. It is much more likely that he spent his days at Montgomery, Clothier & Tyler, learning about the family fortune from his father. The law, per se, was not a profession to which he aspired. He did not have the aggressive, competitive drive of his father. He was more of a people person, with a gentleness and *joie de vivre* that inspired friendships. He also wanted a family. Three children were born at Georgian Terrace over the next ten years: my father, Sidney Frederick Tyler, in 1907; Molly Elkins Tyler in 1910; and George Frederick Tyler, Jr. in 1915. While GFT settled into a routine in the family firm, learning the brokerage and underwriting business,

10. Stella Elkins Tyler as a young mother

Stella, with plenty of domestic assistance, raised the children.

These were halcyon years for the family. In Elkins Park, they were close to other Elkins families. Their home was large enough to entertain lavishly. Servants were on hand to care for the children if necessary and there was no limit to the funds available for clubs, hobbies, and entertainment. GFT was able to pursue his sports interests—fox hunting, golf, tennis, shooting—and both parents were able to escape to Maine and other destinations on George Elkins' elegant yacht, *Juniata*. Captained by a seasoned veteran of the British Royal Navy, *Juniata* had five staterooms and a saloon. It was large enough to sail just about anywhere, and its captain reveled in speed and eccentric maneuvers. Unfortunately, he underestimated the currents when attempting a landing on Hope Island off the coast of Maine, ramming into the rocks, and severely damaging his command. The boat was eventually repaired and donated to the Navy at the beginning of World War I. It had given great pleasure to the Elkins and Tyler families

11. Juniata yacht in Cape Cod Canal, 1915

before the accident, and it had also served the purpose, along with his Newport summer experiences, of persuading GFT that he wanted to sail his own yacht.

Consequently, the first of two schooners he would own was built at Salisbury, Maryland, in 1916. It was described as a long, rakish craft, whose design and construction indicated a movement by yachtsmen back to sails.

GFT joined the Corinthian Yacht Club of Philadelphia. Founded in 1892, it was described by Thomas D. Bowes, et al., in *Later Days of the Corinthian Yacht Club*. Bowes and fellow members viewed the club as the "product of men native to an area bounded on one side by the Delaware River and on the other by a heritage of values that separates the real from the superficial with consummate precision." An exclusive organization, the Corinthian was expected to provide "a comfortably neutral atmosphere in which people can engage in the pursuit of being people without risk of being diverted from that purpose by the intrusion of elements of their environment." In other words, members of the Corinthian expected to be able to enjoy their privileged status without interference from the riffraff. What they feared more than anything was the accusation from others that they were, in some manner, pretentious. Consciously, Bowes concluded, "the physical club must represent the antithesis of that word."

However they were perceived by others, the club was headquarters for the finest yachts owned by the wealthiest Philadelphians. GFT's father became a member in 1897 along with the Van Rensselears, Drexels, Clarks, du Ponts, Lippincotts, Wetherills, Whartons, Montgomerys, Elkins, and other Old

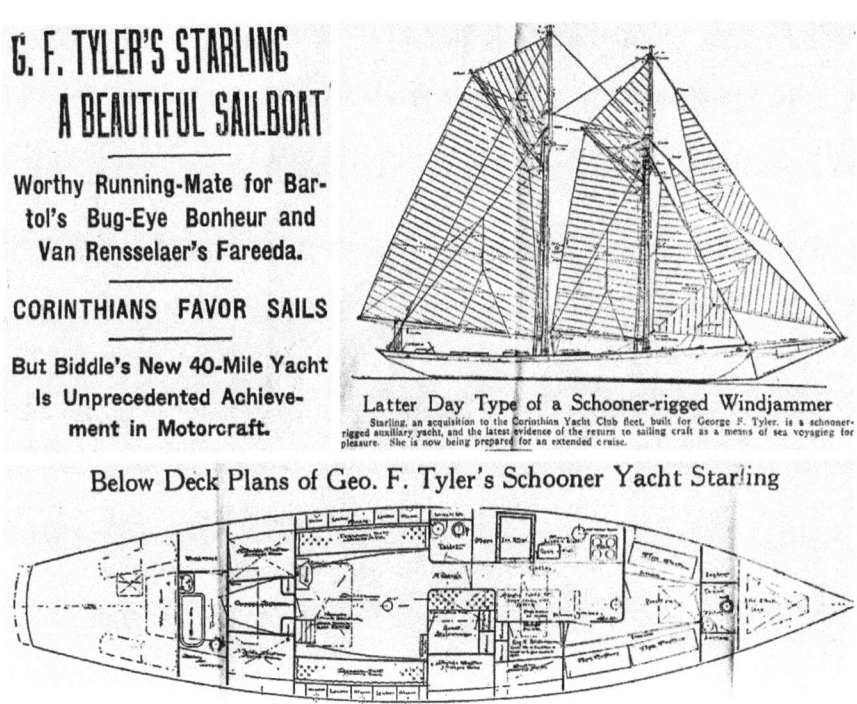

G. F. TYLER'S STARLING A BEAUTIFUL SAILBOAT

Worthy Running-Mate for Bartol's Bug-Eye Bonheur and Van Rensselaer's Fareeda.

CORINTHIANS FAVOR SAILS

But Biddle's New 40-Mile Yacht Is Unprecedented Achievement in Motorcraft.

Latter Day Type of a Schooner-rigged Windjammer

Starling, an acquisition to the Corinthian Yacht Club fleet, built for George F. Tyler, is a schooner-rigged auxiliary yacht, and the latest evidence of the return to sailing craft as a means of sea voyaging for pleasure. She is now being prepared for an extended cruise.

Below Deck Plans of Geo. F. Tyler's Schooner Yacht Starling

12. Starling I design sketches in Philadelphia Record, 1916

Philadelphians. Beginning with thirty-six yachts of all classes, averaging forty-six feet from stem to stern, the Corinthian Club grew in membership, while the average size of the yachts increased in length by ten feet as of 1938. GFT's *Starling I* measured eighty-four feet stem to stern. In every sense, his schooner-rigged windjammer was seen as very competitive with George E. Bartol's *Bug-Eye Bonheur* and Alexander Van Rensselear's *Fareeda*. With 3,000 square feet of canvas, *Starling I* was the best of its class. It provided GFT with the pleasure of enviable ownership along with a degree of absolute control, the likes of which he was unable or unwilling to assert at Georgian Terrace.

Stella ran the show in Elkins Park. From my father's

recollections of the ten years prior to the outbreak of World War I, it is apparent that she was actively engaged as a role model and director of her children's lives. She demonstrated extraordinary discipline at the piano, setting an example for practicing and playing. She took her children to plays, insisting that they read the printed version one time before or after the performance. She required that they learn horsemanship and understand opera, and she taught manners by taking them to visit friends for tea. She and GFT also took them abroad, where they learned about different cultures and historical events. Before returning home on a 1913 trip, they visited the country home of the de Reisets in Osny, France. The caretaker had not been advised of their pending visit, so the visitors were unaware of a series of snares and traps that were in place to ward off poachers. The tripwires were connected to triggers that would fire shotguns if tripped. While bags were being unloaded from the car, Stella took a walk through the gardens, where she still enjoyed warm memories of her time with the de Reisets. Inadvertently, she stepped on a hidden wire and was shot in the head. All but one of the small pellets was removed, but that one ball, too deep in her cranium to be safely removed, remained in place for the rest of her life. Stella healed, but the lead poisoning she may have experienced over time could easily have contributed to certain personality disorders she experienced during the majority of her married life.

The outbreak of World War I and GFT's participation with the American Expeditionary Force changed their lives significantly. Although GFT did not see combat, he returned from France with a different perspective of what he wanted from life.

CHAPTER III:
World War I and the Twenties

Woodrow Wilson was elected president in November 1912. He was inaugurated in March of 1913; during the remainder of the year, he led fellow Democrats through a series of progressive reforms that alienated conservative, upper-class elites. Duties on imports were reduced; a national income tax was passed following approval of the 16th amendment; a Federal Reserve System was put in place to effect banking and currency reform; and the Clayton Antitrust Act was enacted to break up monopolies. The following year, Wilson led the charge to create an eight-hour workday for railroad workers. He raised income and inheritance taxes, and supported an anti-child labor law. All of these measures created a certain amount of hostility amongst the very rich.

When Archduke Ferdinand was assassinated at Sarajevo on June 28, 1914, the existing European alliances responded with declarations of war: France and Russia against Germany and the Austro-Hungarian Empire. When Germany invaded Belgium in August 1914, Great Britain joined France and Russia. World War I had begun.

Most Americans supported Wilson's neutrality and were hopeful the country could remain out of the conflict. The president believed that neutrality would allow the United States to broker a peace, but events of the next two years made that position untenable. Germany placed a blockade around the British Isles, using submarines and mines to keep out commercial vessels from other nations. On May 7, 1915, after a well-publicized warning from the German government that Americans choosing to sail the Atlantic did so at their own risk, the *Lusitania* was torpedoed off the coast of Great Britain with the loss of 128 American lives. Vessels from other countries with Americans on board were also sunk, and even though Germany apologized and committed to ending unrestricted submarine warfare, the attacks continued. To make matters worse, Germany was urging Mexico to attack the United States. When Pancho Villa led an offensive against the little town of Columbus, New Mexico, in March 1916, it became clear that the United States would have difficulty staying out of the conflict.

Wilson began moving away from neutrality, but his party was slow to come around. Vice President William Jennings Bryan resigned in protest, while Protestant churches and women's groups urged the president to stay out of the war. Wilson's successful reelection in 1916 resulted partly from his isolationist foreign policy, but Congress passed the National Defense Act that same year and powerful bankers, industrialists, lawyers, and scions of prominent families became increasingly vocal regarding the need for the United States to prepare for war. They stressed the importance of an expansion in troop strength and naval vessels. The war in Europe served as an epiphany for many of the rich and powerful to argue the need for an enlargement of America's military.

The Plattsburg Movement, born in the summer of 1915, was a result of their actions. Based in New York, it was designed to create an officer corps that was trained and ready for war. GFT was part of this movement. He enlisted in the Officer Reserve

Corps on May 12, 1917, a little over a month after Wilson asked Congress for a declaration of war. He trained at historic Fort Niagara, located on the US-Canadian border at the mouth of the Niagara River, which connected Lake Erie and Lake Ontario. This location had been of great importance during the 18th-century French and Indian Wars, and it had been controlled by both the British and the French until 1796, when the United States took possession. The fort's buildings were old and cold, but GFT and Stella joined with the Benjamin Franklin Peppers, another upper-class Philadelphia family, to rent a house nearby.

GFT graduated after three months of training with a commission as first lieutenant in the army. He was assigned to the 79th Division located at Camp Meade, Maryland, on August 27, 1917, and told to report to Headquarters Company, 311th Field Artillery. On February 1, 1918, he was ordered to the War Department in Washington, D.C., where he was assigned to Assistant Secretary of War, Benedict Crowell. In March he was promoted to the rank of major.

The GFT family moved to Washington and rented a house. In July GFT was ordered to report to General John J. "Black Jack" Pershing's headquarters in Chaumont, France, approximately 170 miles southeast of Paris. On July 5, 1918, he sailed first class on the RMS *Aquitania*, a recently constructed ocean liner belonging to the Cunard Line. When the ship docked at Liverpool on England's west coast, GFT immediately reported to the base hospital. He wasn't feeling well, but he continued on to Brest, France, and thence to Chaumont to report for duty as part of Pershing's G-2 (military intelligence) section.

13. GFT's ID card while serving in the AEF
under General Pershing

G-2's job was to develop counterespionage plans. The American Expeditionary Force (AEF) under Pershing resisted Allied suggestions of amalgamating fresh American soldiers into their depleted and exhausted units. Pershing believed that for the sake of morale it was better for the Americans to fight the enemy under their own command, even though he was warned that racial and ethnic diversity in the AEF could make things easier for German spies. Some Europeans believed that American soldiers with German, Prussian, Austrian, or Hungarian ethnicity might be more vulnerable to enemy propaganda. Pershing was a tough commander, but he was highly respected for his military experience from the Indian Wars to the battles against Spain in

Cuba and the Philippines. He had also led the punitive expedition against Pancho Villa following the raid on Columbus, New Mexico. He was confident that soldiers in the AEF were no more susceptible to enemy propaganda than any other men in Allied units.

At Chaumont, GFT operated under General Dennis Nolan, head of Combat Intelligence at General Headquarters. He was tasked to provide information on enemy operations, beginning work on July 23, 1918. Because he spoke French and already understood the basics of military aviation, GFT was of considerable importance to Pershing, who had taken a keen interest in the value of aerial reconnaissance as he planned the two battles that, for all intents and purposes, ended the war: the Somme Offensive (August 8, 1918 to November 11, 1918) and the Meuse-Argonne Offensive (September 26, 1918 to November 11, 1918). In the United States, GFT had been integrally involved in the Lafayette Flying Corps as early as 1916. This group of wealthy Americans supported their own countrymen who ultimately integrated abroad as pilots with the French Escadrille. The Flying Corps paid for training and equipment prior to the flyers' embarkation to France.

Unfortunately, GFT was not able to remain with Pershing's staff for a celebration of the armistice of November 11, 1918. He was sent home in the middle of October, arriving at Ellis Island on October 25, 1918. He was suffering from chronic pyelitis, most probably the same kidney infection for which he had earlier sought treatment in Liverpool. He was placed in Debarkation Hospital Number 1, where he remained for 4–6 weeks. When he was cleared to return home to Elkins Park, a lethal influenza virus at the Philadelphia Navy Yard was working its way along the coast. Six hundred sailors were infected in Philadelphia, which soon became the city with the highest death toll in the United States. Between October 1918 and March 1919, Philadelphia lost 16,000 people and had 500,000 cases of the flu. Many of the city's doctors and nurses had been called away to war, leaving the hospitals short-staffed for this emergency. All beds were filled in thirty-one available hospitals. Dead bodies piled up on porches and in the streets. Death was everywhere. It is truly remarkable that GFT did not become a victim. He was honorably discharged from the army on December 30, 1918. The malfunctioning kidney was removed at Abington Memorial Hospital.

As brief as it was, GFT's military experience had a profound impact on the remainder of his life. For some unexplained reason, he applied for severance pay and was awarded a paltry $170. The army concluded that he was zero percent physically disabled and therefore not entitled to more than a minimum payment. Psychologically, however, GFT was a changed man. He was very proud of his military service and was active in the Military Order of the Foreign Wars of the United States, the Military Order of the Loyal Legion, and The Military Order of the World War. And when the armistice was celebrated in Philadelphia, he proudly wore his uniform to share in the festivities. He also collected more than 1,500 World War I posters, which were donated to Temple University in 1937.

He was also Pennsylvania's State Commander of the American Legion. The Legion was organized in Paris in 1919 in

14. GFT as Army officer

response to the perceived threat of Communism. In the United States, the Legion also served as a way to provide veterans with education and medical support. According to its charter, the Legion promoted "red-blooded Americanism that will stand against forces that would hamper the growth of the nation." GFT was elected state commander of the Legion, a post he held until 1920.

Given the long-standing Tyler family tradition of service in the nation's wars, GFT felt an obligation to do his part. But as my father noted in *A Joyful Odyssey*, he began to see his own life differently after military service, and with advice from doctors that he slow down a bit to avoid stressing his single kidney, he decided not to return to the competitive world of business. He wanted a less stressful way of life, and he had the assets to create the peace and quiet he sought for himself and his family. He kept his directorship at the Philadelphia National Bank, served on the board of the Fidelity Philadelphia Trust Company, and continued a connection to Montgomery, Clothier & Tyler, but his enthusiasm was directed at finding a country home.

The search began in 1919, four years after the birth of a third child: George Frederick Tyler, Jr. Bucks County, Pennsylvania, was the locus of his search. It was a bucolic community of small farms with deeds dating back to the 18th century. Through the war years, farmers had been encouraged to increase the amount of land in production. Prices for corn and wheat rose exponentially. But when Europe began to recover, commodity prices dropped as fast as they had risen, and small farmers who had borrowed to expand their productivity were having to deal with increased debt and significantly reduced income. Their situation worsened each year during the decade of the Twenties. When they became aware of someone driving a fancy car around the area, looking for property to purchase, the struggling farmers showed interest.

15. Solly Farm House, circa 1965

GFT gave his agent the responsibility of negotiating a fair deal, fearing that farm prices would escalate if potential sellers knew that he was behind the offers. He was especially enamored of a place owned by Theodore and Kate Solly. They had no children to inherit the land, so when they learned that there was an offer contingent on their two neighbors also agreeing to sell, they went to work and secured the necessary commitments. Because he wanted sufficient land to hunt and farm in isolation from others who sought the serenity of the countryside, GFT purchased six additional farms on the west side of Neshaminy Creek, along with the old Spring Garden Mill. In all likelihood, he would have been content with these purchases, but when GFT learned that plans were in the offing to build homes on the east side of Neshaminy Creek, he bought eleven more farms on that side, most of them for $1,000 an acre. Properties west of Neshaminy Creek were called Neshaminy Farms; those east of Neshaminy Creek were Indian Rock Farms. With the passage of time, all of the farmed area was referred to colloquially as Neshaminy Farms.

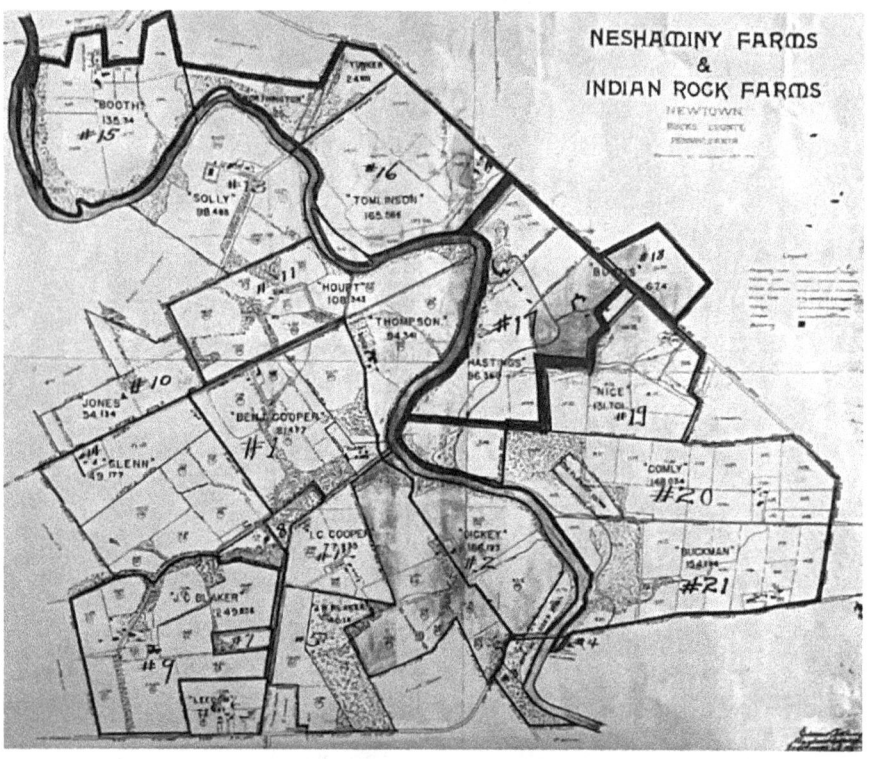

16. Map of Neshaminy Farms and Indian Rock Farms, 1931

In total, he acquired 2,000 acres, comprising what is now the home of Bucks County Community College and Tyler State Park. For many of the farmers who sold out, a new opportunity presented itself. GFT had decided to establish himself as a gentleman farmer, with the goal of using science and technology to meet the highest standards of agricultural production. It's hard to know what motivated him in this direction; there weren't any previous experiences in his life that would have served as stimuli for this pioneering endeavor, although his sister was married to a man who had already established a dairy herd, and their example might have inspired him. As my father has suggested, the war experience had somehow made him more aware of the passage of time, and he wanted to do something worthwhile that had never been done before. To accomplish his goals, he needed labor. Many of the same farmers who sold to GFT were given a chance to hire on as Neshaminy Farms employees. GFT lost no time assisting these families in home improvements they never would have been able to afford prior to selling out.

The stage was set for building his own home (Indian Council Rock) on the acreage purchased. But before addressing what would become the largest mansion built in Bucks County, and perhaps the last mansion of its kind built in the United States, it is important to note other postwar activities in which GFT was involved.

Abington Memorial Hospital became a primary focus for him. Connected to this facility through marriage to the family of its founder, George Elkins, GFT served as president of the hospital board beginning in 1928 until his death in 1947. To put this service in perspective, the long-standing Quaker influence in Philadelphia shines nowhere brighter than in the quiet emphasis on good works. The Pennsylvania Hospital, founded by Benjamin Franklin, dates to 1755, and ever since its beginning, most families of note have earned a plaque on the wall indicating some level of philanthropic support and/or participation on its governing board. Other Philadelphia hospitals, like the University, the Jefferson, and the Bryn Mawr, also bask in the social prestige of their boards. As Nathaniel Burt notes when discussing Philadelphia hospitals, "An institution is known by the board it keeps." GFT's service was clearly in the tradition of Old Philadelphia families, but it was also a very personal relationship, which he further demonstrated when Neshaminy Farms began deliveries of certified milk to Abington Hospital.

GFT's board presidency at Abington was more than an honorary position. He was deeply engaged in hospital affairs, where he developed an interest in medical research. Science seems to have been more on his mind than law or business. On May 20, 1935, he wrote a letter to President Roosevelt informing him that the University of Pennsylvania, the Children's Hospital, the University Hospital, Abington Memorial Hospital, and the Philadelphia Department of Public Health had developed a method for preserving blood serum to be used in the prevention and treatment of infectious diseases. Up until now, he wrote, "there has been no means by which serum could be preserved. The importance of its preservation lies in the fact that serums obtained from those who are suffering or convalescing from various epidemic diseases are of the utmost importance in the diagnosis, prevention, study, and treatment of this group." Hopefully, he explained, this research would provide "invaluable aid in the quick control of epidemics of influenza and other infectious diseases, such as scarlet fever and measles." He reminded FDR of the deaths caused by the epidemic of 1918–19, when the death toll exceeded all the battle casualties of World

War I, and he warned the president that new outbreaks of "far reaching proportions" were likely in the future. "I know how frightfully busy you are," GFT concluded, "but [I] believe it would be worth your while if you could set aside an hour, or even half an hour, some day and permit me to bring a group of doctors down to Washington to tell you the story. ... P.S. I spent last weekend in Cambridge."

Three days later, FDR replied, noting that what GFT proposed was "something very close to my heart." Although he was too busy right then to focus on anything other than the legislation in Congress (Social Security, Neutrality Act, Labor Relations Act, Banking Act), he would be available to meet with GFT when Congress recessed. They met in April. GFT spent two nights at the White House. Presumably, the two Fly Club brothers renewed their Harvard friendship and discussed the breakthrough research on epidemic diseases.

GFT's interest in helping those facing unexpected and harmful circumstances can also be seen in his role as head of a group of Pennsylvania volunteers who made up the central division of the Welfare Federation. Their task was to raise money for 20 hospitals, 26 children's organizations, 21 family agencies, 15 nursing and health groups, 22 neighborhood houses, and 13 character-building agencies. The Welfare Federation was created with the intention to renew coordination and discussion between the many groups that served the needy in Philadelphia. As it shifted its role to providing grants and funds to charity organizations, GFT's interests and skills were much in demand. Ultimately, the organization morphed into the United Way.

While his service on boards continued in the tradition of other Old Philadelphians, GFT also pursued personal interests that gave him special pleasure. In 1926 he became a stamp collector, believing that the hobby was also a good investment. By 1940, he had purchased $450,000 (in 1930s dollars) of stamps, which were carefully placed in 45–50 albums. By the late Thirties, however, he became concerned about the situation in Europe and, fearing another war, he decided to convert from stamps to stocks and bonds. He believed that the sale of his collection would qualify for a long-term capital loss. The Internal Revenue Service disagreed, however, so he pled his case before the United States Tax Court. The court seemed to have agreed that GFT's stamp purchases met the "requisite greed" standard, which was often used to determine whether the purchase of stamps was an investment or a hobby. Because he met the government's standard, they only charged him with the responsibility of calculating the cost basis for each purchase made over the preceding fifteen years. Whether or not he complied is unclear. What is clear is that he stood to lose almost a quarter of a million dollars from stamp sales, so he decided that future investments would be in Philco, Dow Chemical, and Warner Swasey. Between 1926 and 1940, he invested approximately $8,000,000 (in that day's dollars) in stocks. This was a mercurial period for the stock market in which the Dow Jones Industrial Average rose to a record peak of 381 in September 1929 and dropped to a low of 41 in July 1932. During that same time, GFT purchased twenty farms, built Indian Council Rock, and ordered the construction of a larger and faster schooner capable of major ocean voyages. The Great Depression did not appear to have much of an impact on the GFTs.

Starling II was considerably grander than *Starling I*. According to the July 29, 1926, *Bath Independent* of Maine, "A 126' steel auxiliary schooner, the largest sailing lot constructed on the Atlantic coast this year, will be launched at Rice Brothers Yard, East Boothbay, August 1. Starling, as this cruising craft will be named … is building for George F. Tyler of Philadelphia from the designs of John G. Alden. Her auxiliary engine will be a Winton Diesel." *Starling II* was a gaff-rigged schooner that had twice the square footage of sail as *Starling I*. It carried 1,500 gallons of fuel and had a crew of four with four motor launches on davits. By this time, GFT had a reputation as a no-nonsense captain who gave orders and took total command, not allowing anyone else to intrude. When plans were being drawn up for this larger yacht, Stella requested that the internal saloon be large enough to hold a grand piano. She got her wish.

17. Starling II *diesel engine*

18. Starling II *main saloon with Steinway grand piano*

19. Starling II *at anchor*

Starling II sailed to Bermuda, Cuba, and up the New England coast to Maine. The GFTs summered in different places, including Dark Harbor and Northeast Harbor on Mt. Desert Island. Stella's brother, William Elkins, had built a colonial revival home in the 1920s at Dark Harbor called Long Ledge. This was a convenient place to stay, but the GFTs seem to have preferred Northeast Harbor, where they generally booked a room at The Elms on Manchester Road. Known as Philadelphia on the Rocks, Mt. Desert Island attracted wealthy and powerful people—Peabodys, Rockefellers, Astors, Fords (beginning with Edsel), and Mellons—along with dozens of luminaries from churches, private schools, universities, and the art world. It was a gilded-age resort to which the rich and famous began arriving at the turn of the century. Summer visitors enjoyed active lives hiking, sailboat racing, playing tennis, and a busy social life. It was said of Bar Harbor that if you wished to stay there, you needed money but no brains; at Northeast Harbor you needed brains but no money; and at Southwest Harbor—redolent of its fishing industry—you didn't need either. Northeast Harbor was known to have a pious Episcopalian community that resisted racing on Sundays while everyone attended services at St. Mary's By the Sea. The community preserves its conservative orientation today and honors its history as a land grant awarded—without authority—to Samuel de Champlain by Louis XIV in the 17th century. As the author Samuel Elliot Morrison wrote in *The Story of Mt. Desert Island*, "Mt. Desert is not merely an island; it is a way of life to which one becomes addicted." By the time the GFTs discovered it, the island had become a destination for summer visitors who comprised a *Who's Who* of academia and the Protestant Church.

While documentary evidence for the sale of *Starling II* has proved elusive, it is likely that GFT sold the schooner in the 1930s when his summertime focus shifted to Neshaminy Farms. According to information acquired by GFT's grandson Michael Tyler, *Starling II* went through several registrations following GFT's ownership and may have ended up as one of the private vessels serving under the Coast Guard during the early years of World War II. With a designated 50-square-mile section of the coast to patrol, each of these many private yachts and fishing vessels searched for German submarines and picked up crews from sunken ships. The Corsair Fleet was disbanded in 1943.

What is more accurately known about *Starling II*'s fate is

that it was sold to a Chilean fisherman, José María Aldunante Ugarte, in 1941. He wanted a fast schooner that he could convert into a lobster boat for the purpose of transporting freshly caught crustaceans 450 miles from the Juan Fernández Archipelago to Quintero, a port on Chile's coast. Speed was important. *Starling II*'s powerful engine, steel hull, double masts, and large sails made it the perfect vessel for Aldunante Ugarte, but getting it ready for the lobsters was painful.

The grand sala, where Stella entertained guests on her piano, became the lobster storage room. The crew's quarters, with their bunk beds and fine sheets, became a repository for salted fish. The fine rugs, silverware, china, and piano all remained on the ship when it entered the fishing business, and for six trips back and forth between the Juan Fernández Archipelago and Quintero, its home port, *Starling II* was the envy of all competition.

Unfortunately, the return trip in December 1943 proved disastrous. The main engine developed mechanical problems, which were only partially fixed, when a severe storm came up from the south, challenging *Starling II*'s ability to progress in heavy seas. As the lights of Quintero came into view on the night of December 31, 1943, the captain gave orders to turn for what he believed was the passageway into port. Somehow, he miscalculated and the keel smashed into an underwater reef. The ship broke into three parts, and out of thirteen on board, only one man survived. In the misty light of New Year's Eve day, the most prominent part of *Starling II,* its bow, could be seen isolated and forlorn, impaled on the rocks with the remains of Steinway's finest scattered all around. Such was the fate of GFT's maritime love affair.

20. Captain GFT with daughter Molly

Fortunately, other projects he directed had far better outcomes. By 1929 the GFTs had selected a place for construction of their French-Norman style mansion. They hired Willing, Sims & Talbutt as designers of their home in which were incorporated characteristics that reflected their travels as well as the travels of others who returned from Europe after World War I with certain ideas regarding architecture styles for the Philadelphia elite. To implement these design and construction ideas, the Elkins family preferred Horace Trumbauer, but the GFTs chose Willing, Sims & Talbutt because they were viewed by many as the premier society firm of the day. Harrison, Mertz & Emlen designed the gardens while the decoration of more than forty rooms was the work of Henry Davis Sleeper of Boston.

Located in a wooded area overlooking Neshaminy Creek, the site was believed to have been used by indigenous tribes for council meetings on the rock ledges overlooking the stream one hundred feet below. From this local lore came the name given to the GFTs' home: Indian Council Rock. Stella's hand in the exterior design and interior decoration is undeniable. Drawing on her experiences in France, the main house was built with walls two feet thick, lined with cork and reinforced with steel rods. There were balconies, towers, terraces, a cobblestone driveway, a garage with a ten-car turntable, and nearby houses for employees. The main building of sixty rooms extended three hundred feet and included a French Rococo reception hall appointed with 18th-century carved oak panels, a music room with two grand pianos, a game room that featured the chirping and warbling of fifty live-imported European birds, a gun room, and a formal dining room painted in warm gold and decorated with 19th-century murals of English hunting scenes. In the basement, below the game room, GFT supervised the installation of a British pub that had been taken apart in England, shipped to the United States, and reassembled piece by piece for the enjoyment of GFT and his guests. Access to the second floor was by way of a round stone staircase. Upstairs, all the bedrooms had baths and fireplaces; some had gold fixtures. Clocks with cuckoos lined a long hallway where a designated servant had the exclusive responsibility of synchronizing all the temperamental mechanisms. Another servant was charged with placing flowers and carafes with fresh water in every room. Nearby gardens were configured to replicate the Jardins des Tuileries in Paris, with various levels and compartments, a variety of flowers and shrubs, and fountains and sculptures. When she first saw the drawings, Stella wondered, with some justification, if the landscape looked too much like Versailles. A swimming pool with bathhouses and two tennis courts (clay and grass) offered exercise and entertainment. A stable of horses was a short drive away.

Construction began in 1930; the GFTs moved into their new home in 1932. The stock market was in free fall, the economy in retreat. For one hundred Italian stone masons, many of whom were from the same family, a year and a half building Indian Council Rock was an unexpected and greatly appreciated job opportunity. The brownstone they used was taken right off the property, so the GFTs did not have the additional expense of trucking rock to the building site. Even so, when all is said and done, the construction of Indian Council Rock and its companion buildings and gardens cost $1,361,000 in 1930 ($23,817,500 in 2021 dollars). By any measure, construction of the largest home ever built in Bucks County, when unemployment in the United States reached twenty-four percent and people without work lived on the streets or in their cars, was a mixed bag of ostentation and opportunity.

21. Indian Council Rock

CHAPTER IV:
Neshaminy Farms

While GFT was buying land and working on plans to establish a farming operation, he was also actively pursuing his memberships and connections within the Old Philadelphia establishment. He remained very much engaged within the social circle in which he grew up. He belonged to the Huntingdon Valley Country Club, the Philadelphia Cricket Club, the Pine Valley Golf Club, the Sunny Brook Golf Club, the University Barge Club, the Rabbit Club, the New York Yacht Club, the Tennis and Racquet Club, the Eastern Yacht Club, the International Sportsmen's Club of London, and the Traveler's Club of Paris. He was also a member of the prestigious Philadelphia Club and the Schuylkill Fishing Company, known also as the State of Schuylkill. The Fish House, as it was nicknamed, was established in 1732 and maintained a membership that for generations represented the wealthiest of Old Philadelphians. As Nathaniel Burt notes in *The Perennial Philadelphians*, "There are clubs, as there are charitable boards, for all, or almost all, but they are organized into a strict hierarchy, too, and firmly and finally at the top are … the Fish House and the Philadelphia Club."

But the difference between GFT and most other Old Philadelphians with whom he and the Elkins family had associated for generations is that GFT wanted to use his wealth to create something new and consequential. Beginning with the purchase of the Solly farm and its two neighboring properties, he began buying dairy cattle. To provide expertise, he hired Dr. Ernest Christian Deubler to oversee the properties and keep the animals healthy. Deubler was a veterinarian who was known to have developed the first brucellosis-free herd of cattle in the nation. He was a devout believer in the superiority of the Ayrshire breed for milk production, and he had an outstanding reputation. GFT gave him full rein to replace the Guernseys he had purchased with Ayrshires. That herd eventually expanded to 230 cows and became known for its quality milk products. The foundation heifers were sold to strengthen other dairy farms all over the country.

As Neshaminy Farms gradually began production of dairy products, wheat, and beef, it became clear that GFT was committed to top-of-the-line people, products, and playthings. In addition to the farm, he sought out and paid for the best yachts, the finest hunting horses, a home that was built and decorated by talented designers and decorators, and surrounding gardens with exotic plants that employed the most skilled gardeners. His pursuit of excellence also applied to automobiles.

In 1933 he purchased a brand new two-seater Pierce-Arrow Model 1242 convertible coupe. This exquisitely designed luxury car had a 264-cubic-inch side-valve L-Head (Flathead) V-12 engine, producing 175 horsepower. It also had a three-speed transmission, a twin-coil Delco-Remy ignition system, Stromberg carburetors, two spare tires nestled in the front fenders, painted wire wheels, a rumble seat, and a fold-down Wexford tan top. At a time when the popular Ford Model A was selling between $400 and $600, GFT's Pierce-Arrow would have been priced around

22. GFT's Pierce-Arrow, 1933

23. GFT's Pierce-Arrow, 2022

$4,500; almost $100,000 in 2021 dollars. The Model 1242 was without question one of the finest cars on the market in 1933. It drove like a dream, its engine running as quietly as the famous Rolls-Royce Silver Ghost. When properly tuned, it was capable of almost 100 mph, representing in many ways Pierce-Arrow's last gasp at greatness. The company had merged with Studebaker in 1928 for the purpose of being able to access cash to build its large engines. But the partnership failed. Studebaker, an enterprise that had been producing transportation vehicles since horse-drawn wagons were popular in 1852, was forced to declare bankruptcy in 1933. Pierce-Arrow was left to compete with Packard, Lincoln, Cadillac, and Marmon, all of which were developing 12- and 16-cylinder engines in order to become the first company selling a car to the public that would attain 100 mph without special adjustments. The challenge for Pierce-Arrow was steep, and it was made a lot worse by the Great Depression. When the company recognized its inability to sell enough cars to remain competitive, Pierce-Arrow closed its doors and went out of business in 1938.

GFT's car is one of three Model 1242 convertible coupes to have survived the past ninety years. Of the three, it is the only one to retain its original engine. Since its sale by GFT's estate in 1947, the car has had a series of owners, residing now with collector Ross Myers of Montgomery County, PA. Given the fact that this vehicle looks about the same today as it did in 1933, with the exception of some new paint and interior upgrades, it remains an outstanding example of GFT's aspiration to own and manage only the highest quality possessions and businesses.

The best example of GFT's exemplary standards for business is Neshaminy Farms. For this project, he needed a superintendent who could oversee all the dairy and farming operations, including the Spring Garden Mill, wheat production, alfalfa and hay operations, as well as planting and harvesting soy beans, corn, oats, and other crops. GFT's good fortune in finding the right person might be described as pure serendipity.

In 1923 Roland "Rolly" Wellington Porter was in his last year of studying engineering at Cornell University. He had taken a break from his studies and was attending a New York City church on a Sunday that Stella happened to visit while on a shopping trip. She arrived late that morning, and Rolly made space for her, providing a hymnal open to the appropriate page. Stella was so impressed with the young man's good manners that she urged GFT to see if he might be available to work for them. The next thing he knew, Rolly was invited to accompany the GFTs on *Starling II* to Maine. He had experienced a difficult relationship with his own father and soon found that, by contrast, he and GFT were extremely compatible. Following the Maine trip, he was invited to accompany the family to Europe for two months, at which time GFT offered him a job as superintendent of all Neshaminy Farms' agricultural operations. Rolly refused at first, afraid that his father might be angry if he didn't finish his degree. But later he changed his mind. He had been in the hospital with a bout of encephalitis and thought the outdoor activities might be good for him. For the next forty years, right up to Stella's death in 1963, he was superintendent and business manager of Neshaminy Farms. Rolly never finished his degree at Cornell, but he made a friendship with the GFT family that proved just as meaningful. Even though his role as rent collector and rules enforcer was at times contentious, he enjoyed his work and was respected by the families who served GFT under his leadership.

24. Rolly Porter at the helm of Starling II

By the time the GFTs moved into their Indian Council Rock home, Neshaminy Farms had become a viable operation. Unfortunately, the local economy was somewhat of a disaster. According to an article by Roger Simon in the *Encyclopedia of*

Greater Philadelphia, as of 1933, only forty percent of the Philadelphia workforce was fully employed. More than half of the banks and loan associations were in default. Philadelphia government was in the hands of an entrenched and corrupt machine, while party leaders and the conservative elite shared Herbert Hoover's *animus* against government intervention and publicly funded charity. This doctrine of laissez-faire led to calls for public relief. Ninety thousand homeowners had already lost their homes, and the depth of the crisis threatened to overwhelm private charity. The New Deal was just beginning to provide assistance, but Republican hostility toward FDR's progressive relief measures, combined with the belief that Communists were gaining power, caused the elites to panic when marches and protests occurred.

We don't know with any certainty how GFT felt about the impact of the Great Depression on the poor, but we do know that the Old Philadelphians in general felt a strong antipathy towards any kind of federal assistance. The funds at GFT's disposal made possible the execution of his wildest dreams, and his social status positioned him squarely in the midst of those who saw FDR as a traitor to his class. There must have been a frequent tug of war waging in his mind. He was FDR's friend and classmate, and he was dedicated to helping those around him who were in need. But he must also have presented himself as being equally shocked at New Deal policies. Poems and newspaper articles in his scrapbooks make fun of FDR and glorified Hoover. But it is more than likely that GFT played a very cagey role, recognizing that he needed the good will of Old Philadelphians when they gathered at

Indian Council Rock for social events that required a charitable donation. Essentially apolitical, GFT seems to have remained solidly loyal to his class, while rewarding his employees, leading efforts to improve the lives of the poor, and raising funds for medical, educational, and social institutions. It would not have been easy for him to assuage the needs of both camps.

Compared to the 250,000 people unemployed in Philadelphia in 1933, farmers working at Neshaminy Farms not only lived with their families in homes that had been modernized at GFT's expense, they also had secure jobs in a dynamic agricultural setting. They no longer owned their own farms; they were tenant farmers. But at a time when so many people from all walks of life were losing everything they had, these families were engaged in the work they enjoyed and were employed by an owner who cared for their well-being. Twenty to twenty-five families received a bottle of milk daily along with turkeys and eggs. Some families lived in their upgraded homes rent-free during periods of financial difficulty. All families could look forward to gatherings at Christmas, Thanksgiving, and midsummer for an outdoor picnic sponsored by the GFTs. Stella invited the children for a pool party when she celebrated birthdays (although she never appeared at these gatherings), and when families had unexpected emergencies, they could count on the GFTs for assistance. In a few instances, employees' children received college tuition. It was a good place to work, and the teamwork of Rolly Porter, Ernest Deubler, and GFT presented a unified drive for excellence that gave Neshaminy Farms a national reputation as one of the finest agricultural enterprises in the nation. Because he wanted the operation to develop stature and respect on its own merits, GFT never used the Tyler name; instead, milk bottles were labeled Neshaminy Farms Dairy. For this and many other reasons, there was a lot of pride associated with being employed by Neshaminy Farms.

25. GFT feeding calves in three-piece suit

The Ayrshire herd grew slowly during the decade of the 1930s. Porter and Deubler focused on the quality and volume of milk from disease-free cows, much of which was certified and delivered to Abington Memorial Hospital. For its emphasis on quality, Neshaminy Farms frequently received the coveted Constructive Breeder Association Award, which signified that the herd had met the highest standards of production and type, with one hundred percent of the cows being bred at Neshaminy Farms. Because the cows were free of mastitis and Bang's disease,

Neshaminy Farms was recognized annually as one of the top dairy herds in the United States and was invited to send two of its top producers to the Borden's Dairy World of Tomorrow, an important feature of the 1939 World's Fair in Flushing Meadows, New York. The herd was also chosen by American Cyanamid Corporation, a manufacturer of agricultural chemicals, as a recommended source of replacement animals for dairy farms across the country.

26. Ayrshire cows at Neshaminy Farms

According to Rolly Porter, GFT was a *doer*, involved in every phase of Neshaminy Farms operations. He wasn't terribly concerned about annual profits, but if Neshaminy Farms made money, it was plowed back into the business. He had a flair for creativity and experimentation, always striving to be the best.

Neshaminy Farms raised Herefords with the same focus on quality. These were purebred animals on which records were kept on birth weights, weaning weights, yearling weights, and many other traits that would be important to commercial cattlemen interested in upgrading their herds. Neshaminy Herefords numbered 500 at one time, many of which were shipped, along with Ayrshire breeding stock, to the West and as far away as Cape Town, South Africa.

Neshaminy Farms wheat was also shipped all over the United States and out of the country, especially after the end of World War II. Deliveries were made to Canada, Switzerland, and Israel. The wheat was considered to be of sufficient quality to satisfy the high standards demanded by Jewish communities for the production of matzoh for Passover celebrations. Rabbis came to Neshaminy Farms to inspect the harvest and processing of wheat before it was purchased by Horowitz and Margareten of Long Island City, one of the largest baking companies in the United States. They rode the combines and oversaw the milling, cleaning, and bagging stages at Spring Garden Mill. With the rabbis' approval, the milled wheat would be purchased and ultimately baked into unleavened bread, which the Jewish community shared as a reminder of what their ancestors ate in their flight from Egypt, the Exodus, the foundation story of the Israelites.

The horses on Neshaminy Farms were as noteworthy as the cattle and wheat. When work on the farm began in the 1930s, most of the power for planting, cultivating, and harvesting was provided by Percherons. There was only one tractor, and it was hard to start. These large draft horses originated in France. Known for their intelligence and willingness to work, they are the fourth largest horse breed in the world. Gradually, Neshaminy Farms converted to tractors, but Percherons remained an important part of GFT's world. He crossbred them with Thoroughbreds, creating a hunting horse that my cousin Winky Lowry, also a grandchild of GFT's, described as a big, safe rocking chair.

GFT was a very good horseman, and he loved riding to the hounds. The stables at Neshaminy Farms were overseen by up to five grooms with the responsibility of twenty-five horses. Huntsmen from the Huntingdon Valley Country Club, including Old Philadelphians from the Elkins, Sinkler, Wharton, Dixon, and Widener families and others came to Bucks County to ride as often as twice a week. They chased foxes all the way to the Delaware River. Occasionally, damage was done to private property, but the sight of riders in red coats and black velvet hats loping through the countryside made memories for everyone. And the property damage was always repaired.

GFT's head groomsman, Orville Reeves, was a man of few words. Having been kicked in the mouth by a horse, Orville smoked a bent-stem pipe as a way to keep his artificial upper teeth in place. He had an excellent relationship with GFT, but he also liked his booze. When he was busted for making moonshine, GFT bailed him out. When his good-looking daughter got into trouble, GFT came to his rescue with financial aid. When Orville needed medical help in his later years, GFT paid the bills. Needless to say, the stables were well maintained and a source of pride for GFT and for Stella as well, who was an equally outstanding horsewoman.

All around what used to be Neshaminy Farms, visitors can

27. Unidentified horses and hounds on a hunt, 1927

still see and appreciate the GFTs' focus on creative landscaping. They enriched the farming operations with purchases of exotic flora and fauna. Agents were sent all over the world to locate rare birds, plants, flowers, and trees, most of which had never been nurtured in Bucks County or in any other part of the United States. As many as 150,000 trees were planted on land that was unsuitable for grains and forage crops. Maples, sycamores, and dogwoods lined the entry road into Neshaminy Farms, enhancing the already picturesque drive along Neshaminy Creek.

In addition to cattle and wheat, the farm managed an average of five thousand ring-necked pheasants in a wire-roofed pen. Ninety percent of these were incubator hatched at Neshaminy Farms. Other pheasants were also raised, along with peacocks, white rats, guinea pigs, and mallard ducks. The birds ate more than three hundred tons of grain a year, and most of them ended up in the possession of local gun clubs. Turkeys were also a large part of the avian industry. Marketed under the business name of Indian Rock Game Farms, these birds were specifically developed to be smaller and stockier, with a larger amount of white breast meat. They weighed less than traditional eighteen-pounders, but they carried as much edible meat. They were so popular that orders came in from September through April. On the average, 2,500 birds were sold and shipped all across the country. Geese and mice (for medical research), and peacocks were raised along with pigs and sheep. Two chicken farms provided eggs and meat for employees and local residents, and those farmers who needed grain for their livestock could count on deliveries from Spring Garden Mill. As Rolly Porter recalled, Neshaminy Farms had "two grain trucks on the road every day during winter months," both of them hauling discounted feed to neighboring farmers. There was plenty of work to go around, but employees also took the time in winter to organize sleigh rides and engage in the thrilling sport of skijoring.

When GFT died in 1947, Neshaminy Farms was at the peak of its success. Instead of a plaything for a rich family, the farm had earned a reputation as an enterprise on the cutting edge of agricultural research and production. But with GFT's death, the driving force was gone. Rolly Porter stayed on as manager as long as Stella lived on the property. Employees continued doing their jobs; awards came in regularly. But as soon as Stella passed away in 1963, the 2,000 acres and the resident farmers gradually morphed into something entirely different and equally impressive: Bucks County Community College and Tyler Park.

CHAPTER V:
GFT's Legacy

Several theories may explain the cause of GFT's death on January 8, 1947, at the age of 63. In *A Joyful Odyssey*, my father describes the younger GFT as a fun-loving extrovert who thoroughly enjoyed life. But he was changed significantly by the horrific pain he suffered as a result of a malfunctioning kidney, and when he began to recover after its removal, he was forced unexpectedly to deal with the onset of Stella's mental health problems. Although she remained for the most part a lovely, talented, and generous person, her behavior became increasingly erratic, perhaps a result of lead poisoning caused by the one remaining pellet in her brain from the accident in France. It is also possible that her manic-depressive, bipolar personality was simply a result of genetics. Because she frowned on taking medication, her mercurial behavior was occasionally extreme. What were described as "moods" became increasingly difficult to manage. GFT's forbearance was limitless, but the onset of such a radical change to Stella's normally gentle temperament saddened him and may have contributed to his early demise. Her conduct may have influenced him to drink more, smoke more, and isolate himself. On the death certificate, his doctor listed the cause of death as advanced coronary arteriosclerosis along with aortic stenosis. He had plaque buildup in his arteries, most probably a result of high cholesterol, and a narrowing of the aortic valve, producing a reduction of blood flow from his heart into the main artery. Most likely, the drinking and smoking contributed to his heart failure, but the sorrow he felt as a result of Stella's personality disorder must have been devastating and equally debilitating.

28. GFT and Stella at their son George's wedding, 1937

In his will, GFT left everything to Stella. When his estate was probated in December 1947, it was described by the December 13 *Bristol Courier* as "the largest appraisement and inventory in the history of Bucks County": $3,102,349 ($37,228,188 in 2021 dollars). A lot of his assets were already in trust for his wife and three children, and therefore not counted in the appraisal. But not Neshaminy Farms nor Indian Council Rock, both of which subsequently ended up in good hands as a result of Stella's philanthropic generosity and her executors' decision to embrace the public good.

Stella and GFT had already donated Georgian Terrace to Temple University in 1939. This gift, valued at $1,000,000 ($20,680,000 in 2021 dollars), was specifically designated to serve as the first home of the Stella Elkins Tyler School of Fine Arts. By the time of GFT's death, Stella was becoming a recognized sculptress under the tutelage of Boris Blai, who was hired as the founding dean of the new school. His teaching philosophy, according to Roberta A. Mayer in *Stella Elkins Tyler: A Legacy Born of Bronze*, evolved from the time he spent as a soldier fighting for the French in the trenches of World War I. Through his daily experiences of fear, he learned to find calm by filing pieces of shrapnel into figures. He became convinced that using one's hands to make art had the power to relax the body and quiet frayed nerves. When he began teaching at the Oak Lane Country School of Temple University, he and Stella became acquainted. The passion for sculpture he showed at Oak Lane inspired Stella to hire him as her teacher. They worked mostly in clay with an emphasis on the nude female body, and as Stella became more productive, the frequency of her "moods" decreased, and her level of "happiness" increased. In Mayer's words, "Blai had taught her that happiness—and well being—derived from using one's hands. Tyler was delighted by the attention and grateful that this work gave her such satisfaction."

29. A happy Stella at age fifty-three (right) with unidentified woman, 1937

30. Stella sculpting in her studio at Indian Council Rock

By the end of World War II, the Stella Elkins Tyler School of Fine Arts was beginning to outgrow the forty-five rooms and ten acres of Georgian Terrace. On December 1, 1950, almost four years after GFT's death, Stella, already a ten-year member of the Temple board of trustees, proposed to gift Indian Council Rock and 200 acres to the university, believing that they could either establish a branch campus or transfer the School of Fine Arts to Bucks County. The only reservation she requested was the right to "use, occupy and enjoy the whole of the property during her lifetime." The board accepted her offer. In her 1960 will, the boundaries of the gifted property were described in a formal survey, and when she died on November 2, 1963, Temple accepted the property, understanding that her executors had one year to dispose of her personal possessions.

Temple trustees soon decided, however, that Indian Council Rock would not be manageable. About the same time, the Bucks County Board of Commissioners voted to fund a two-year college. They had not yet selected a location, and when they learned that Temple was looking for a buyer for Indian Council Rock, they passed a resolution on June 22, 1964, that provided the legal authority to purchase the property. The Pennsylvania State Board of Education approved it; on January 29, 1965, the newly elected Bucks County Community College (BCCC) trustees purchased Indian Council Rock and 200 surrounding acres that stretched between Neshaminy Creek on the west and Swamp Road on the east. They paid a very reasonable $700,000. The first class of students arrived in September 1965. With three campuses available today, eighty programs of study, a number-one ranking for online courses in Pennsylvania, and tuition holding at under $8,000 after financial aid, BCCC is a bargain and a powerful legacy attributable to the GFTs' generosity.

The future of what was once Neshaminy Farms (1632.9 acres) was left to the wisdom of Stella's beneficiaries: my father Sidney, my uncle George, and my aunt Molly Tyler West. Stella

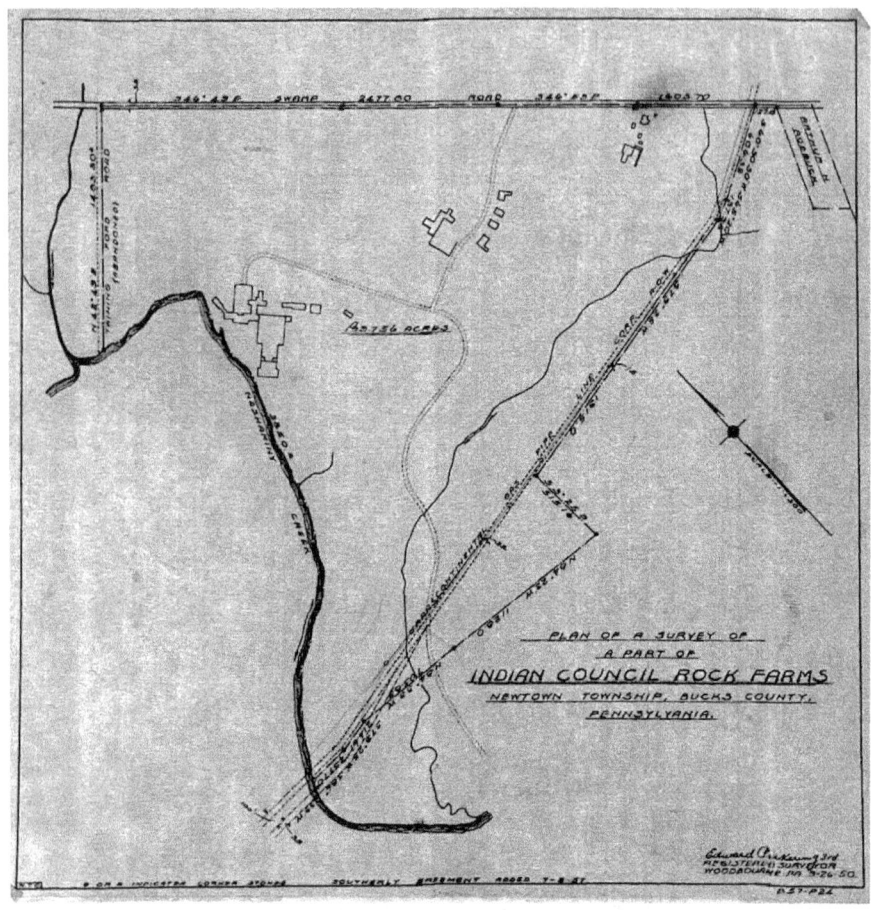

*31. 1950 Survey of 200 acres given to Temple University,
now Bucks County Community College*

left an estate valued at $2,121,892 ($20,264,068 in 2021 dollars) according to a Montgomery County inventory, but this amount did not include the bulk of her assets which were stocks already tied up in trust. As trustees of Stella's estate, Sidney, George, and Molly, along with the Philadelphia-Fidelity Trust Company, had to agree on whether the 1632.9 acres should be sold to the highest bidder for the construction of private homes or sold to the Commonwealth of Pennsylvania for use as a public park. Five developers had already made tantalizing offers, but the executors, to their credit, decided to sell the farm land at a reasonable price to the Commonwealth of Pennsylvania, provided the appropriate enabling legislation could be passed. The State was given one year —1964—to get this done.

From a historical standpoint, the creation of Tyler Park happened as the result of circumstances that can only be seen as another serendipitous event. In 1963, before Stella's death, the people of Pennsylvania were asked to vote on a referendum that if passed would authorize the Department of Forests and Waters to spend up to $70,000,000 on the acquisition of land for the purpose of state parks, reservoirs, conservation, recreation, and historical preservation. Fifty-three percent of voters approved what was referred to as Question 3, a legislatively referred constitutional amendment. Known as Project 70, this amendment passed on November 5, 1963, three days after Stella's death. In order for the state to purchase any lands, the legislature would have to approve enabling legislation.

When Sidney, George, and Molly realized that Neshaminy Farms might qualify as a state park under Project 70, they made known their interest in negotiating a sale. If they showed or felt any impatience with the Commonwealth, it was because they knew how slowly bureaucracies move. A quick and lucrative sale was already a possibility from eager developers. The money realized from this land, if sold for development, would have been considerably more than what it was worth as farmland sold to the state. There is no way to know how the siblings interacted during their discussions of the best way forward, but it's more than likely that there were strong opinions expressed on both sides.

Ultimately, they reached an agreement that favored a sale to the Commonwealth of Pennsylvania, and on June 22, 1964, in a special session, the legislature surprised everyone by passing the Project 70 Land Acquisition and Borrowing Act. The wishes of the voters were now enshrined in formal legislation, but Pennsylvania still had to approve an enabling act that would give the state power to borrow the necessary money. In 1964, farmland in Bucks County was valued at $790 an acre. However, Bucks County was experiencing a population boom. All land values were rising precipitously. In *Philadelphia Inquirer* articles written in the summer and fall of 1964, it was noted that the 1946 assessed value of Neshaminy Farms land was $3 million. It's not clear how that figure was calculated, but the agreement reached between trustees and the state in 1964 was seen as a steal. "Without the sympathy of the trustees," noted the state's negotiator, "we could never have been able to acquire the land. If the tract had been subdivided and sold to developers, it would have brought much more than the state will pay for it." The price agreed to by both sides was $1,182 an acre for a total purchase price of $1,930,000.

On November 23, 1964, the Commonwealth of Pennsylvania entered a Declaration of Taking in the Bucks County Recorder of Deeds Office. This tactic, also referred to as a friendly condemnation or eminent domain action, is used to avoid a transfer tax and other fees. In December, the trustees executed a release of the deeded land that included an agreement that the state would pay $500,000 immediately and the balance due of $1,430,000 on or before July 31, 1965.

Tyler State Park was born. It was the second property purchased by the state under the Project 70 Land Acquisition and Borrowing Act. It has served its purpose as an accessible public recreation area, but the transfer from farming to public recreation took ten years. Rolly Porter stayed on to oversee that transformation. It was not easy. Even though the dairy operations and chicken farms had long since been shut down, farmers were still planting soy beans, corn, wheat, and barley. Livestock continued to graze the meadows and haying operations functioned as in the past. Transition to a viable public facility required some farmers to leave, others to work out lease arrangements. These were challenges Porter had to deal with as the business of agriculture gradually morphed into the creation of a large public recreation area. Bathroom facilities needed to be built along with trails for hiking, biking, and horseback riding. Signs needed to be posted with safety regulations and directions to the picnic areas, the 36-hole disc golf course, the covered bridges, the old grist mills, and other places of historic importance. As Brian Rounsavill points out in his well-researched *The History of Tyler State Park*, it wasn't easy to persuade the Commonwealth that some of the old buildings had historic value and needed to be preserved. In his words, "They felt that the farm buildings did not directly contribute to park operations and there was no funding available for their ongoing maintenance and rehabilitation." They looked at Tyler State Park as open space; buildings were unnecessary. But the local community disagreed, and with the organization of Friends of Tyler Park, an arrangement was worked out whereby some tenants could remain in their homes with the understanding that on a year-to-year basis, their upkeep on these historic properties could be evaluated. Many structures were eventually leveled, but ten buildings remain, some dating back to the 18th century.

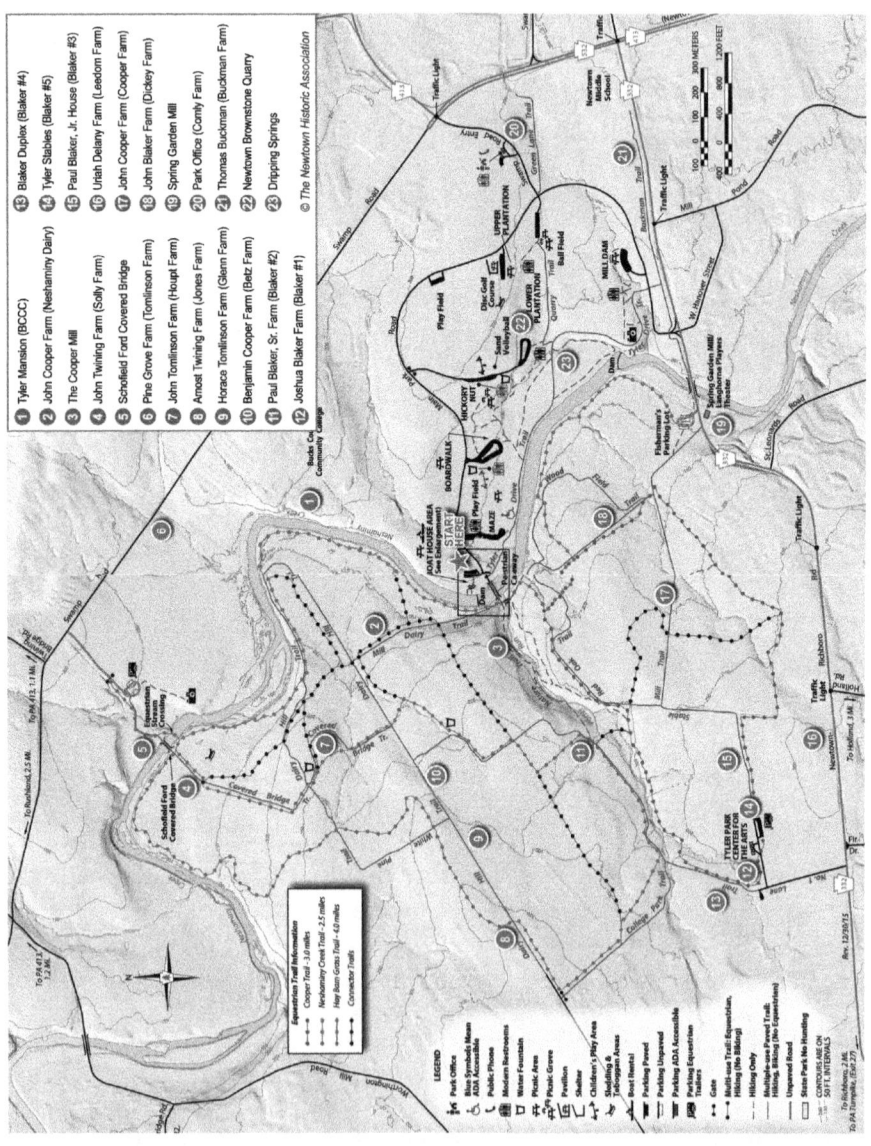

32. *Tyler Park showing some of the farms purchased by GFT*

Tyler State Park was dedicated and opened to the public on May 25, 1974. As Rounsavill notes, along with the open spaces, Neshaminy Creek, picnic areas, and other playgrounds, the property boasts more than 23.5 miles of interconnected trails, with environmental education and interpretive programs "exploring a variety of ecological topics." It is a true gem for the citizens of Bucks County and for thousands of others who come from all over to enjoy the legacy of George and Stella Tyler.

Management of the Park comes with the challenge of dealing with different cultures and varying conditions, such as the COVID-19 pandemic. Recently, some visitors have taken over sections of the Park, violating policies on alcoholic beverages, noise limitations, swimming in Neshaminy Creek, parking regulations, and general behavior not in concert with the hoped-for peaceful appreciation of the Park's natural beauty. This is to be expected with a population that is more mobile, more diverse, and often looking for ways to let off steam. It can be an irritant, but behavior is controllable with proper oversight and education. The beauty of the Park itself and the incredible value resulting from the Tylers' desire to share their good fortune with the community cannot be tarnished by a few irresponsible individuals.

GFT and Stella were generous with their wealth. They took steps to assure that a large portion of their assets would be put to work for future generations of their family. But at the same time, as can be seen in their connections to Temple University, Abington Memorial Hospital, Children's Hospital, the Philadelphia Orchestra, and other organizations, as well as the employees who worked for them, they used much of their wealth to benefit the public. Bucks County Community College and Tyler State Park serve as very visible evidence of this extraordinary philanthropy.

A month after GFT died, the *Abington Memorial Hospital News* included a commentary titled, "George F. Tyler As We Knew Him." The words therein appropriately testify to a life of service to others:

We, of the hospital family, knew of his position in the business world and of the many activities in which he was engaged, and [we] respected him for thus having made his mark among his fellow men.

But we had even greater respect for him, because he was our friend. He was a friend—to trustees, doctors, nurses and hospital employees. No problem of theirs was ever too small—or too large—for his consideration, and he was always ready with a helping hand for the people he loved.

He was a friend to the people of the community—most of whom will never know how much they owe to this man, who labored tirelessly so that the finest hospital and medical care would be available for those who needed it.

Being President of an institution as large as Abington Memorial Hospital and directing its activities so that it could be of real service to the community, was no easy job. It required long hours of thought and study, attendance at innumerable meetings and complete knowledge of all phases of the hospital's activities. ... He served term after term, not for any glory or prominence to be attained but because he felt that in his way he could be of service to the community at large.

No record can ever adequately chronicle his contributions of time, effort and funds to the hospital, and through it, to the community.

The passing of George F. Tyler, our friend, was a severe shock and he will be missed by all of us. We are grateful, however, for having known him and for having been able to call him our friend.

GFT's death was a shock to everyone; he was only 63. But life expectancy of a white male born in 1883 was 47. According to that statistic, he had lived a full life, and he experienced a timely death. Even so, he had become such a loyal friend to so many people in so many different organizations that his demise caused a feeling of great loss. In a way, it is this very genuine, human, and gentle side of GFT that distinguished him and fed the grief of those with whom he worked. Given his background, he could have been aloof and demanding, but that wasn't his essence. For Abington Hospital to refer to him as a "friend" was really a very high compliment, and I believe that he would have smiled with considerable satisfaction had he been able to read the hospital's testimonial.

33. GFT in 1937 at his son's wedding

CONCLUSION

It is tempting to conclude that this journey into my grandfather's life and circumstances has settled the angst associated with knowing how privileged the Tylers were during the Great Depression. Unfortunately, the original question raised by brother Sid and myself is still haunting: How can any family spend such enormous sums of money on every aspect of luxury when large numbers of people are dying from a basic lack of food and shelter? The answer, I now believe, is that GFT and Stella were first and foremost Philadelphia Brahmins. They were connected to other families with similar educations, wealth, and upbringing. They were accustomed to doing things on a grand scale, and their lives were so insular that they were relatively unaware of the degree of social and economic devastation occurring around them. They entertained lavishly, spent summers at posh resorts, traveled abroad first class, owned classic pieces of European art, sent their children to the best private schools, drove around in chauffeured Cadillacs, and lived in a French-Norman mansion cared for by dozens of servants. Theirs was a life of leisure, made possible by the enormous wealth passed down to them by previous generations.

This is not to say that they were oblivious to the sufferings of others. Nor do I wish to imply that their philanthropy was anything less than bold and generous. They cared deeply about other people and institutions, and they demonstrated their altruism constantly in a myriad of ways throughout their respective lifetimes. But they were both born into privilege and believed that whatever they did for themselves, or for others, should be done at the highest level, whether for work or for play or for humanitarian interests. Money was simply not a concern.

In fact, neither Stella nor GFT were even remotely interested in making money. They didn't have to. But neither did they obsess over the need to shelter and grow their own fortune for the exclusive benefit of their children. They wanted their heirs to do well, but they also wanted each of them to *do* something and not just *be* somebody.

In sum, they combined the perquisites of wealth with a desire to achieve goals that would ultimately make a difference in the lives of their fellow citizens. They wanted to leave a mark on society, and they seem to have succeeded, as seen in the creation of a renowned school of art, a community college, a public park, a first-class research hospital, and a multitude of investments in the lives of individuals who benefited from their compassion and generosity.

Stella and GFT did their *doing* for different reasons and under different circumstances. Early on, Stella showed her disdain for the formalities of traditional debutante life. The two years of schooling in France that she chose as an alternative to coming-out parties made possible a worldly education and countless opportunities to hone her artistic sensitivities. As with most imaginative people, she cultivated an innate desire to be unique. Indian Council Rock and its gardens, which have been such a boon to Bucks County Community College, were a direct result of her personality, her travel, and her education. In France she had developed high standards in music, art, and design. Her instinctive sense of creativity was nurtured there, and when she began life as a married woman, she applied those standards to her own home and estate. As her emotional issues grew more concerning, she focused on sculpture. It gave her purpose and helped calm the destabilizing aspects of her bipolar condition. It also gave the public a look at the work of an expressive and fertile artist.

GFT's *doing* evolved gradually. He was changed by the war years. Losing a kidney was part of the reason he sought a less stressful life away from the Philadelphia countinghouses. But he was also impacted by the experience of military service, where he met and interacted with many capable men and women whose upbringing was far less privileged. It would be impossible to prove that he developed a greater respect for everyday people during his two years in uniform, but the possibility can't be ruled out. We can only say with certainty that he managed Neshaminy Farms with great sensitivity to the needs of his employees and, as Abington Hospital acknowledged, he made time for all who sought his guidance. The same could be said for his work with the Boy Scouts of America, the American Legion, the Westminster Choir, and other organizations to which he gave his time.

As a result of their wealth, both Stella and GFT seem to have felt a responsibility to society: *noblesse oblige*. While it may seem awkward to compare their privileged lives to those of regular people who suffered so much during the Great Depression, the fact remains that the GFTs put a lot of people to work and they saved many who might otherwise have been victims of the economic collapse. One might contend that they could have done a lot more. I would find no fault with that argument. But compared to the rest of the Philadelphia gentry, they did pretty well. Furthermore, in pursuit of both their personal and professional interests, they created an ongoing legacy that stands today, not just in bricks and mortar, forests and glens, but in a graceful way of life that might serve as a model for any generation. GFT was a gentleman. In his behavior towards others, he represented by example the chivalric code of 15th-century knights: humility, gratitude, courage, justice, generosity. Stella was equally the lady. Together they set an example that would be most appropriate today. Especially today. They both understood the meaning of honor, courtesy, and grace.

Like almost all Old Philadelphians, GFT was not an aristocrat in the true sense of that word. He had no interest in governing, and neither did most of his social class. He was more Hamiltonian than Jeffersonian, and he disdained the idea that government could or should interfere with his freedoms. But he also felt deeply about his country, and he believed that he had an obligation to participate in her defense when called, just as his ancestors had answered the call in previous wars and insurrections. He was proud of the Tyler military record and disappointed that the family's application for membership in the Society of the Cincinnati was rejected. The nation's oldest patriotic organization, founded in 1783, honors those who fought with General Washington. Unfortunately, the family ancestor Captain Daniel Tyler of Brooklyn, Connecticut, who made a name for himself fighting with the General, was a militiaman, not regular army. For this reason, the several attempts by various members of the Tyler family to join the Society have been rejected.

As with most human beings, there are inconsistencies in GFT's life that make characterization a challenge. But there is also enough evidence to say with assurance that he was a very decent person who used much of his inherited wealth to improve the quality of a major industry. While it is not uncommon for members of an upper class to contribute to philanthropic causes and dabble in business, GFT's commitment to Neshaminy Farms as a first-class operation is a noteworthy accomplishment. More often than not, his peers were too frequently content to be gentlemen members of boards and social clubs. They tended to cling to the past in a world they saw as too eager for the future. But GFT embraced the future. Through livestock raising, wheat farming, and milk production he aimed to set new quality and production standards. Ultimately, his search for excellence saw fruition when Neshaminy Farms' acquired an international reputation.

As I wrap up this brief view of my grandfather, there is a wry smile on my face as I now see that his life was an amalgam of Old Philadelphian and entrepreneur. I suspect that for those born into great wealth, it is quite difficult to part with the comforts associated with the culture. Kudos to GFT! He was comfortable in the role of country squire, and his children were infused with many of the ingredients of that Weltanschauung. My own father carried on in that tradition. He, too, opted for a life of *doing* after serving in the military. Moving his wife and five children from Pennsylvania to a ranch in Colorado in 1946 was seen by some friends and family as a radical step. And it was! But as with GFT, my father wanted to start something on his own that would benefit his family and utilize his business skills. He had no idea how the West differed from the urban East. And he didn't even know which end of a horse gets up first (the front). But he learned on the job and was always pleased when the Crystal River Ranch actually completed a year in the black.

Becoming a successful rancher wasn't easy. Having grown up in the privileged environs of Georgian Terrace, St. Mark's School, and Harvard College, my father was conditioned to see the world in a certain way. The somewhat Victorian views of society he inherited occasionally landed him in difficulties with the Colorado locals. But he toughed it out, never losing his manners or his principles, and when he began to feel comfortable as a ranch owner whose calves were winning prizes at the Denver Stock Show, he allowed himself the luxury of building a tennis court, in full view of ranch operations, where players were admonished to wear white. For me, his teenage, wannabe-cowboy son, it was a total embarrassment. But now I know that like GFT before him with his fox hunting, skeet shooting, and expensive cars and boats, a certain amount of conspicuous consumption was permissible. Gentlemen, after all, need a sense of pride in what they *do*.

I can say now that I like GFT. I wish I had "known" him. I think I understand him better for having tried to flesh out his life, and I think he deserves applause for who he was and what he did, immersed as he was in a very select group of privileged human beings.

RIP, GFT. *Esse Quam Videri.* TO BE rather than TO SEEM TO BE, indeed!

ACKNOWLEDGMENTS

I received valuable assistance from family members Carol Tyler, Michael Tyler, ChrisTyler, Toby Tyler, Robert O. Tyler, Stella (Winks) Lowry, and Carol Tyler Noble. Some shared pictures; others read versions of early drafts. All encouraged me, for which I am most grateful.

I was also aided by Caroline Blackburn, a professional researcher who worked many angles to help me locate GFT's war record as well as the documentation that showed how Tyler Park was created. Phil Schmidt, Manager of Tyler State Park, Jeff Marshall, Executive Director of the Heritage Conservancy, and Brian Rounsavill, an officer in the Newtown Historic Association, were instrumental in critiquing the manuscript and providing Bucks County-oriented data. Margaret Sager of Heckscher, Teillon, Terrill & Sager provided me with a copy of my grandmother's will and Margery Sly, Director of Temple University's Special Collections Research Center, opened up old board meeting minute books for me so I could better understand my grandmother's handoff of property to that institution. At Bucks County Community College, I was assisted frequently by Monica Kuna, who rallied her colleagues to help me whenever I had an archival question. And Scott Laughlin, who has studied the history of old Philadelphia homes and their residents, shared his knowledge and contacts with me.

Finding anyone with memories of Neshaminy Farms when it was a working operation was difficult, but Virginia Reynolds, daughter of farm manager Roland Porter, and her daughter, Cheri Beckman, were actively engaged in finding pictures and other contacts for me, as well as films Porter made during his tenure on the farm.

Bert Lippincott of the Newport Historical Society, Andrew States of the Bucks County Community College Foundation, Daniela Accetura of the Northeast Harbor Archives, and Lisa Shaw, steward of the Fly Club at Harvard University, were helpful when I needed specific information on GFT. Juliana Kuipers, Senior Development Collection Curator/Archivist at Harvard University's Pusey Library, went out of her way to help me find GFT's four-year academic record at Harvard. Brent Merrill, onetime owner of GFT's 1933 Pierce-Arrow convertible coupe, and Ross Myers, present owner of the car, were a great source of information.

Two people who have made this a better work are Lyle Rosenberger and Dawn Petersen. Lyle has been intent on preserving the history of Indian Council Rock, especially its gardens, and as much of the Tyler legacy as possible. His 2011 book *Tyler Elegance: A Garden Odyssey* is a gem. In addition to teaching his craft to students, he has strongly influenced employees in the way they see and value the Tyler heritage. He has been especially generous to me during the several years this book has been in the making, and I feel indebted to him for his steady hand and wisdom. Dawn has provided the technical editing skill that any manuscript requires prior to publication. But over and above that service, she has made every effort to get into my head, ask tough questions, and offer both advice and constructive criticism. She has taken a rough structure and streamlined it with consummate skill. To Lyle and Dawn, I am deeply grateful.

PHOTOGRAPH CREDITS

1. The Newtown Historic Association, Inc Archives.
2. The Howard Diers Collection, Atlantic Publishing and Engraving Company of New York, 58.19.254.
3. Sidney F. Tyler, *A Joyful Odyssey, Part 1*. S.F. Tyler, 1990.
4. David Nelson Wren, *Ardrossan: The Last Great Estate on the Philadelphia Main Line*. Bauer and Dean Publishers, 2017.
5. Sidney F. Tyler, *A Joyful Odyssey, Part 1*. S.F. Tyler, 1990.
6. Fly Club Archives, Harvard University.
7. Harvard University Archives, UAV 170.270.7 Folder 20.
8. Roberta Mayer, *Stella Elkins Tyler, A Legacy Born of Bronze*. Bucks County Community College, 2004.
9. Carol Noble.
10. Sidney F. Tyler, *A Joyful Odyssey, Part 1*. S.F. Tyler, 1990.
11. U.S. Naval History and Heritage Command, NH 76410.
12. *Philadelphia Record*, January 2, 1916.
13. Carol Noble.
14. Sidney F. Tyler, *A Joyful Odyssey, Part 1*. S.F. Tyler, 1990.
15. The Newtown Historic Association, Inc Archives.
16. The Newtown Historic Association, Inc Archives.
17. Morris Rosenfeld, NY. Carol Noble.
18. Morris Rosenfeld, NY. Carol Noble.
19. Morris Rosenfeld, NY. Carol Noble.
20. Carol Noble.
21. Chris Tyler.
22. Brent Merrill.

23. A. Ross Myers.

24. Virginia Reynolds.

25. Carol Noble.

26. Carol Noble.

27. *New York Herald Tribune*, December 25, 1927.

28. Bucks County Community College Foundation Archives.

29. Bucks County Community College Foundation Archives.

30. Bucks County Community College Foundation Archives.

31. Pickering, Corts & Summerson, Inc.

32. Michael DiFiori and The Newtown Historic Association, Inc.

33. Bucks County Community College Foundation Archives.

SOURCES

Books:

Baltzell, E. Digby. *Philadelphia Gentlemen: The Making of an Upper Class*. New Brunswick and London: Transaction Publishers, 1971 and 1979.

Barrie, Robert. *Early Days of the Corinthian Yacht Club of Philadelphia*. Philadelphia: John Spencer, Inc., 1940.

Bowes, Thomas D., et al. *Later Days of the Corinthian Yacht Club*. Philadelphia: John Spencer, Inc.,1967.

Burt, Nathaniel. *The Perennial Philadelphians: The Anatomy of an American Aristocracy*. Philadelphia: The University of Pennsylvania Press, 1963.

Cooke, James J. *Pershing and His Generals: Command and Staff in the AEF*. Westport, CT: Praeger Publishers, 1997.

Davis, Allen F. and Mark H. Haller, eds. *The Peoples of Philadelphia: A History of Ethnic Groups and Lower Class Life, 1790–1940*. Philadelphia: Temple University, 1973.

Doty, James L. III. "With a Little Help From Our Friends: The Development of Combat Intelligence in the American Expeditionary Forces, 1917–1918." Dissertation, Ohio State University, 2010.

Encyclopedia of Greater Philadelphia. A digital resource produced by the Mid-Atlantic Regional Center for the Humanities at Rutgers-Camden. See www. philadelphiaencyclopedia.org.

Forrey, William C. *History of Pennsylvania's State Parks: 1984–2015*. Bureau of State Parks, Office of Resources Management,

Department of Environmental Resources, Commonwealth of Pennsylvania, Harrisburg, PA, 1984.

Garrison, James B. *Houses of Philadelphia: Chestnut Hill and the Wissahickon Valley 1880–1930*. New York: Acanthus Press, 2008.

Hall, James Norman and Charles Bernard Nordhoff, eds. *The Lafayette Flying Corps*. Boston and New York: Houghton Mifflin Company, 1920.

Historical Branch, War Plans Division, General Staff, "Brief Histories of Divisions, U.S. Army, 1917–1918," June 1921.

History of the Seventy-Ninth Division, A.E.F During the World War: 1917–1919. History Committee, 79th Division Association. Steinman and Steinman: Lancaster, PA, 1922.

Larson, Paul H., Kevin I. Burge, and Keith L. Barr. *The First Wings of War. Air Force Reserve in World War I*. Air Force Reserve History Program, Robins Air Force Base, Warner Robins, GA.

Leach, Josiah Granville. *Genealogical and Biographical Memorials of the Reading, Howell, Yerkes, Watts, Latham, and Elkins Families*. Reprint of a volume printed or in private circulation by J. B. Lippincott Company of Philadelphia, 1898.

Mayer, Roberta A. *Stella Elkins Tyler: A Legacy Born of Bronze*. Newtown, PA: Bucks County Community College, 2004.

Morison, Samuel Eliot. *The Story of Mount Desert Island*. Islandport, ME: Islandport Press, 1960.

Noble, Richard E. *The Echo of Their Voices: 150 Years of St. Mark's School*. Hollis, NH: Hollis Publishing, 2015.

Pershing, John Joseph. *My Experiences in the World War*. New York: Frederick A. Stokes Company, 1931.

Rounsavill, Brian. *The History of Tyler State Park: A Self-Guided*

Historical Walking Tour. Newtown, PA: The Newtown Historic Association, Inc., 2021.

Social Register. New York: The Social Register Association, various dates.

Tyler, Norman. *15 Generations of American Stories. Notable Descendants of Immigrant Job Tyler*. Ann Arbor, MI: Norman Raymond Tyler, 2019.

Tyler, Sidney F. *A Joyful Odyssey: Part One*. Tucson, AZ: Sundance Press, 1990.

The Tyler, Elkins and Allied Families: A Genealogical Study. Compiled for George F. Tyler. New York: The Lewis Historical Publishing Company, 1939. Digitized microfilm version at the Family History Library, Salt Lake City, UT.

Welcome to Tyler Hall, Bucks County Community College. Bucks County Community College Foundation, Rita Melamud, designer, n.d.

Newspapers:

Philadelphia Inquirer

Newtown Enterprise

Philadelphia Record

Bar Harbor Times

Bath Independent

Delaware County Daily Times

Bucks County Courier Times

Doylestown Daily Intelligencer

Bristol Daily Courier

New Castle News

Hanover Evening Sun

Online and Archival Sources:

Bigelow, Michael E. *A Short History of Army Intelligence* by the Command Historian for U. S. Army Security and Intelligence Command, https://fas.org/irp/agency/army/short.pdf.

Ruffin, Steven. *The Lafayette Escadrille*. E-Book, 2016-05-19. https://www.google.com/books/edition/The_Lafayette_Escadrille/XeA1DgAAQBAJ?hl=en&gbpv=1&printsec=frontcover.

Incoming Passenger Lists, 1917-1938, NARA, Records of the Quartermaster General, 1774-1985, Record Group 92, Box 103.

American Battle Monuments Commission, Chaumont Marker, AEF Headquarters, https://www.abmc.gov/Chaumont.

The Medical Department of the United States Army in the World War, Vol. V, Military Hospitals in the United States, Lieutenant Colonel Frank W. Weed, M.C., U.S. Army, Government Printing Office, Washington, 1923.

U.S. Army Medical Department, Office of Medical History, Chapter XXII, Embarkation and Debarkation Hospitals. https://history.amedd.army.mil/booksdocs/wwi/militaryhospitalsintheus/chapter22.htm.

Find a Grave Index, database, *Family Search*. https://www.familysearch.org/ark:/61903/1:1:QVGP-47C9 : 2 July 2020, Sidney Frederick Tyler, 1935; Burial; citing record ID, Find a Grave.

National Register of Historic Places Inventory Nomination Form for George F. Tyler Mansion, United States Department of Interior, 16 July 1987.

Barnard, Charles H. and John Jones. "Farm Real Estate Values in the United States by Counties, 1850-1982." Washington, D.C., U.S. Department of Agriculture, Economic Research Service, 1987.

Marsching, Major J. H. "History of the Army Intelligence School," After Action Report, c. March 1919, National Archives Record Group 120, Carton 1737.

Temple University, Special Collections.

Northeast Harbor, Library and Archives.

Mount Desert Island Historical Society, Mt. Desert, ME.

Islesboro Historical Society, Islesboro, ME.

Harvard University Archives, Pusey Library.

The Historical Society of Pennsylvania.

The Denver Public Library.

ABOUT THE AUTHOR

Daniel Tyler is a retired history professor. Born before WWII, he grew up on a ranch in Colorado prior to studying at Harvard College. After receiving a degree in political science and a commission in the USAF, he served as a jet flight instructor and taught history in Hawaii. Tyler returned to ranching for a few years then earned a Ph.D. in American History. He taught in Mexico, Argentina, and at Colorado State University where he researched the West's water development and resulting conflict. Previous publications by Daniel Tyler include, "The Last Water Hole in the West," "WD Farr, Cowboy in the Boardroom," "Silver Fox of the Rockies," and "Love in an Envelope."